Dr David Clutterbuck has written or co-authored more than 20 management books, including the best-selling *The Winning Streak*. In recent years, he has focused on quality themes, becoming the recognised European expert on service quality strategies and carrying out a variety of research projects to identify best practice in empowerment. He also acts as a consultant to major UK and international companies.

Chairman of The ITEM Group plc, senior partner of business research consultancy Clutterbuck Associates and director of The European Mentoring Centre, David Clutterbuck holds academic posts at Putteridge Bury and Sheffield Business Schools, in addition to the International Management Centres. He was founder editor of the management journals *Issues, Marketing Business* and *Strategic Direction*; he also launched Tom Peters' newsletter, *On Achieving Excellence* in Europe.

WHAT THE EMPOWERERS HAVE TO SAY:

'To free someone from rigorous control...and to give that person freedom to take responsibility for his ideas, decisions, actions, is to release hidden resources that would otherwise remain inaccessible to both the individual and the organization'
Jan Carlson, former CEO of SAS Scandinavian Airline System

'We finally figured out that for every pair of hands we hire, we get a brain for free, so why not use it?'
Anonymous CEO

'Make every decision as low as possible in the organization. The charge of the Light Brigade was ordered by an officer who wasn't there looking at the territory'
Robert Townsend, former CEO, Avis

'The age of the hierarchy is over'
James R. Houghton, Corning chairman and chief executive

'We likened an empowered team to an orchestra in which management provides the music, the team leader acted as conductor and the team members as the highly skilled instrumentalists'
Brian Howes, President of Kimberly Clark's Service and Industrial Sector

WHAT THE EMPOWERED HAVE TO SAY:

'We all have more responsibility for the job now...packers have the power to say: "this product isn't good enough, I'm not packing it"'
Hazel Mayo, packaging operator, Walkers Smiths, Snack Foods

It doesn't matter whose name is on the gate, because this is my company'
Jimmy Howerton, an associate at Ericsson GE

'What did it cost? Just our brain power'
Walkers Smiths, fryer operator

'I take the projects I work on very seriously now. I feel if projects don't succeed, I haven't succeeded. So I'll move mountains to make sure they work'
Andrew Tyler, Marine Scientist, British Marine Technology

'I like my job more than I ever used to. I do better work, I make more money'
Ocelia Williams, line employee, Cine Made Inc.

The POWER of EMPOWERMENT

Release the Hidden Talents of your Employees

David Clutterbuck
and
Susan Kernaghan

With research by Debbie Snow

KOGAN
PAGE

81869

First published in 1994
Paperback edition published in 1995

Apart from any fair dealing for the purposes of research or private
study, or criticism or review, as permitted under the Copyright,
Designs and Patents Act, 1988, this publication may only be
reproduced, stored or transmitted, in any form or by any means,
with the prior permission in writing of the publishers, or in the case
of reprographic reproduction in accordance with the terms of
licences issued by the Copyright Licensing Agency. Enquiries
concerning reproduction outside those terms should be sent to the
publishers at the undermentioned address:

Kogan Page Limited
120 Pentonville Road
London N1 9JN
© Clutterbuck Associates, 1994

British Library Cataloguing in Publication Data

A CIP record for this book is available from the British Library.

ISBN 0 7494 1049 3 (Hardback) ISBN 0 7494 1752 8 (Paperback)

Typeset by Saxon Graphics Ltd, Derby
Printed in England by Clays Ltd, St Ives plc

Contents

FOREWORD

The power of empowerment

This book has its origins in a sense of mounting frustration. Management fads come and go – I have probed and promoted enough of them over the past 20 years to recognize that, in most cases, they are simply new ways of looking at what every effective manager already knew, but could not necessarily articulate or systematize. Each new concept develops rapidly beyond its originator's perception, taking on something of a life of its own as different people add their own interpretations.

Empowerment has suffered this maturation process at a galloping pace – so much so that it is almost impossible to gain any kind of rational consensus as to exactly what it is. In visiting companies around the world, I have encountered organizations that perceive empowerment to be a total dismantling of the managerial structure in favour of a semi-egalitarian ideal; companies that consider empowerment to be little more than delegation; and others that see it simply as an element of some other change programme, such as total quality management, where employees are empowered to do what they have to, to meet customers' needs, but have either little or no influence on other critical issues that affect their jobs.

The arguments behind these different interpretations of empowerment are equally diverse, but usually include some reference that indicates that the whole process is as beneficial for employees as for the company. This view is not always shared by the employees themselves. All too often, empowerment can simply mean shouldering more responsibility for less reward. In these cases, employees rarely find themselves empowered to say 'No'.

Indeed, it may not be fanciful to wonder whether the victims of empowerment outnumber the beneficiaries. Even at middle management levels, while theory says that sharing power increases it, the reality may often be that the manager is empowered entirely out of a job.

It's not surprising, then, that I should hear from people at all levels in organizations expressing a frustration in understanding both what empowerment *is* and what it *should* be. To try to impose a standard definition upon empowerment would be akin to trying to stabilize the Queen's English – impracticable and probably undesirable. But trying to understand the processes at work and record some aspects of good practice did seem to be both practical and useful. That is what we have set out to do in this book.

In constructing both the best practice research and the book itself, we inevitably debated whether the term 'empowerment' was not in itself an impediment. After all, some very successful international companies, such as British Airways, have opted instead to talk about 'taking responsibility', to avoid confusion about their aims. Yet all the alternatives we discovered were equally capable of multiple interpretation. In the end, we concluded that it probably doesn't matter what name you give this particular rose, as long as it helps people to:

❏ take more control over their jobs and working environment

❏ enhance the contribution they make as individuals and members of a team

❏ seize opportunities for personal growth and self-fulfilment.

The manner in which an organization may approach these tasks will vary according to culture and circumstances, but we have taken the view that empowerment is a goal, rather than a process or technique. Viewing empowerment in this light makes it easier to reconcile it with the multitude of preceding 'new' management techniques, such as semiautonomous work groups, quality circles and 360-degree appraisal. All of these seem to have a part in empowerment, but cannot encompass the whole.

Another way of looking at empowerment is as a syndrome consisting of many possible symptoms, only some of which will appear in each organization's approach.

From the dozens of companies with which we discussed the nature of empowerment, we have extracted four critical common characteristics of success. These are:

❑ having a clear concept of what you mean by empowerment (or whatever name you give the empowerment objective) and articulating that concept clearly and widely to employees at all levels – and, in many cases, to customers, too

❑ being totally honest about the reasons for investing time and resources into what in most organizations will be a major change of culture, systems and infrastructure

❑ being realistic about the amount of effort and commitment it will take and the length of time needed

❑ genuinely wanting these changes to come about – recognizing and fervently believing that they are essential to the long-term viability of the organization.

In this book, we first attempt to bring some clarity to the different perceptions of empowerment and the basic principles that underlie it. Then we look at some of the most important building blocks – organization structures, team-working and approaches for changing the behaviour of both managers and front-line employees. We take a special look at empowerment in the service sector, before examining how you can empower yourself. Finally, we demonstrate different shapes of empowerment through case studies of companies in the United Kingdom, Europe and the United States.

Some of the most successful examples of empowerment I have seen (for both the organizations and the individuals who worked in them) have been in pioneering small companies as much as two decades ago. For instance, the small Australian electronics company, where the employees as a whole decided between them what jobs should be done and by whom; and settled each other's salaries. Or the Californian retailer, where employees decided personally how much they should be paid and how much time off they should take. The challenge today is how to extend such high-trust, high-commitment cultures into organizations employing hundreds or thousands of people. As our cases show, it *is* possible. However, it takes time, supreme effort and a great deal of temporary discomfort. The empowerment rose, too, has its thorns. If grasping the rose doesn't hurt, then it probably isn't having much effect!

1
WHO NEEDS EMPOWERMENT?

Empowerment is the corporate equivalent of the fountain of youth.
Management writer Peter Kizilos[1]

When I hear the word empowerment, I reach for my gun. It's like new bottles for old wine.
Bernard Taylor, Professor of Business Policy at Henley Management College[2]

Oh those words! Empowerment? Nonsense! They need to know what their jobs are.
W. Edward Deming, a founder of TQM

INTRODUCTION

In November 1993, Kevan Robinson, a cooker operator at Walkers Smiths Snack Foods in Lincoln, stood up before an assembly of company managers and asked for £25,000 to install a new auto flavouring belt on his team's production line.

Studies carried out by Robinson's team of operators had established that the new machine would improve the quality, and hence the marketability, of the snacks they made.

Projects like this set Robinson and his colleagues apart from the vast majority of factory workers, most of whom use more skill driving to and from work than at any time during the working day. A vast amount of innovation, intelligence, and what Walkers Smiths packaging machine operator Geoff Tempest calls 'free brain power', remains untapped in industry. Most companies still squander it in a way they would never dream of if they were wasting tangible raw materials.

Companies are slowly waking up to the benefits of developing and empowering their staff. Results of the 1993 Employment in Britain survey suggest that in some areas at least, British employees are feeling more empowered than they were even a few years ago. Sixty-three per cent of employees surveyed reported that the level of skill they use in their jobs has increased in the last five years, while 70 per cent said they influenced routine decisions regarding the amount and quality of their work and substantially more than in 1984 said that they were involved in decision-making about their work tasks. Not surprisingly, employees surveyed said they were more satisfied with the outcomes of technical and organizational changes when they were directly involved in the decision-making process.[3]

However, this new-found influence does not seem to have extended as far as workers would like it to. Only 32 per cent of employees responding to the survey felt they could exert influence over broad changes in the way their work was organized and 49 per cent thought they should have more say in this kind of decision.

A recent survey of American workers[4] elicited similar responses. It found that, while 64 per cent of respondents believed their companies were encouraging empowerment, 86 per cent were of the opinion that business leaders failed to practise what they preached.

WHAT IS EMPOWERMENT?

Part of the problem with understanding and implementing empowerment is the difficulty of defining precisely what empowerment is.

Richard Carver, managing director of the Coverdale Organisation, defines empowerment in terms of encouraging and allowing individuals to take personal responsibility for improving the way they do their jobs and contribute to the organization's goals. It requires the creation of a culture which both encourages people at all levels to feel they can make a difference and helps them to acquire the confidence and skills to do so.

Other definitions we have found helpful include:

❑ finding new ways to concentrate power in the hands of the people who need it most to get the job done – putting authority, responsibility, resources and rights at the most appropriate level for each task

❑ the delegation of responsibility for decision-making as far down the management line as possible

❑ the controlled transfer of power from management to employee in the long-term interest of the business as a whole

❑ creating the circumstances where people can use their faculties and abilities at the maximum level in pursuit of common goals, both human and profit-oriented

❑ the psychological energy that activates us.

What is power?

Views on empowerment are confused by lack of clarity on what power is and how we should regard it. Jeffrey Pfeffer of the Stanford Business School suggests that while power has long been a dirty word, it is actually the only way to get things done in an organization. He ascribes the inability to get things done, to have ideas and decisions implemented, to the misallocation and misuse of power. He maintains:

> By pretending that power and influence don't exist, we contribute to what I and some others see as the major problem facing many corporations today, particularly in the United States – the incapacity of anyone except the highest level managers to take action and get things accomplished. You have to concentrate power in order to use it, but in most companies, power is concentrated at the top, away from the front line where it is most useful.[5]

According to Richard Carver:

> Power lies with the people – it is not something that can be delegated down from senior management. Empowerment is a

process of setting the right environment and structure in which people can make a full contribution with the best of their skills. Traditionally, the way we work in Britain has been to impose constraints from above, but empowerment recognizes that there is power and authority everywhere within an organization and the trick is to free it for effective use.

It is not, however, always comfortable for those who are empowered. They cannot say, 'It's not my fault the plant burnt down, because I did as I was told'. By freeing people, we are asking them to take a greater measure of responsibility.

'Most people agree on what power is: the ability to get things done, to get people to do what you want, to make the final decision, but if the boss exercises power less directly these days, how does he make sure things get done and done right?' asks Thomas A. Stewart, associate editor of *Fortune* magazine. 'Where does power accumulate when hierarchies are flattened or when an organization is decentralized? The tyrannical chief executive may be on the way out; the new boss is a nicer guy. But is he less powerful?'[6]

According to Stewart there are five basic kinds of power:

❑   the power to reward

❑   the power to punish

❑   authority: power that goes with the job, the power to veto, the power to sign £1,000 cheques

❑   expertise

❑   referent power, which attaches to a leader because people admire him

Richard Carver suggests a sixth type, which he calls 'process power' – the power that individuals have which allows them to make helpful interventions in interactive processes.

Jane Halpert, a professor of industrial and organizational psychology at Chicago's de Paul University, points out that the first three powers – reward, punishment and authority – come with the office. The higher your rank, the more power you usually have, but expertise and referent power inhere in the person. They can exist anywhere in an organization. The best leaders, she says, use personal power.

According to Stewart:

> This trend away from exercising power based on position and toward using the personal kinds seems to be the new direction of corporate America. The power to reward is increasingly circumscribed ... and punishments can't be used promiscuously on a mobile workforce.
>
> Real power comes from giving it to others who are in a better position to do things than you are. The idea behind sharing power more broadly is to move decisions as close as possible to where action can be taken. Not to spread power around, but to pinpoint it. The decisions that result are faster and cleaner, so more decisions can be made and more work done. There's a big difference between power that is decentralized and power that is diffused, as in a local planning commission, where many people can say no, but it's unclear who can say yes.[7]

Like an electricity grid, power in organizations is rarely concentrated in a single individual or group of people. Even in a heavily centralized organization, smaller concentrations of power emerge throughout the network – often as defensive walls against encroachments from the centre.

Power flows within the network too, as authority is delegated for a task, or as external circumstances imbue parts of the organization with greater influence. For example, the marketing function tends to become more powerful when business is going well; finance when it is going badly.

In an empowered organization, one of the aims is to ensure that power:

❑ is never 'locked up' in one or two parts of the organization

❑ is able freely to flow where and when it is needed.

At its extreme, the analogy with the electricity utility is one of 'who turns the lights on?'. Is it appropriate for a householder to ring the utility to ask it to switch on the kitchen lights, or for the householder to flick the switch him or herself?

HOW DOES IT WORK?

David E. Bowen, an Associate Professor of Management at Arizona State University, and Edward E. Lawler, Director of the Center for Effective Organizations at the University of Southern California, have done extensive work comparing the performance of empowered versus conventional, production line, organizations.

They define empowerment as sharing with front-line employees four organizational ingredients:

1. information about the organization's performance

2. rewards based on the organization's performance

3. knowledge that enables employees to understand and contribute to organizational performance, and

4. power to make decisions that influence organizational direction and performance.[8]

In a production line approach, these features tend to be concentrated in the hands of senior management. With an empowerment approach, they tend to be moved downward to front-line employees. Empowerment, even by this definition, can range from giving staff a suggestion box, to asking them to run the company without managers.

Bowen and Lawler define three types of empowerment:

1. **Suggestion involvement** represents a small shift away from the control model. Employees are encouraged to contribute ideas through formal suggestion programs or quality circles, but their day-to-day work activities do not really change. Also they are only empowered to recommend; management typically retains the power to decide whether or not to implement any ideas they generate.

    'Suggestion involvement can produce some empowerment without altering the basic production line approach,' say Bowen and Lawler. 'McDonalds for example listens closely to the front line. The Big Mac, Egg McMuffin, and the McBLT all were invented by employees. Florida Light and Power, which has won the Deming Quality Award, defines empowerment in suggestion involvement terms.'

2. **Job involvement** represents a significant departure from the control model because of its dramatic opening up of job content. Jobs are redesigned so that employees use a

variety of skills. Employees believe their tasks are significant, they have considerable freedom in deciding how to do the work, they get more feedback than employees in a command and control organization and they each handle a whole, identifiable piece of work.

However, despite the heightened level of empowerment that it brings, the job involvement approach does not change higher level strategic decisions concerning organization structure, power and the allocation of rewards. These remain the responsibility of senior management.

3. **'High involvement'** is a third level, a form practised by Federal Express, Semco Brazil and the now famous Johnsonville Foods of Sheboygan, Wisconsin.

High involvement organizations give their lowest level employees a sense of involvement not just in how they do their jobs, or how effectively their group performs, but in the total organization's performance. Virtually every aspect of the organization is different from that of a control-oriented one. Information on all aspects of business performance is shared horizontally across the organization, as well as up and down the (delayered) structure.

Employees develop extensive skills in teamwork, problem-solving and business operations and participate in work unit management decisions. High involvement organizations often use profit sharing and employee ownership.

According to Bowen and Lawler:

Higher involvement designs can be expensive to implement. Perhaps most troublesome is that these management techniques are relatively undeveloped and untested. People Express, for example, tried to operate as a high involvement airline, and the ongoing struggle to learn and develop this new organizational design contributed to its operating problems.

Today America West is trying to make high involvement work. New hires spend 25 per cent of their first year's salary on company stock. All employees receive annual stock options. Flight attendants and pilots develop their own work procedures and schedules. Employees are extensively cross trained to work where they are needed. Only time will tell if America

West can make high involvement work as it struggles with its financial crisis stemming from high fuel costs and rapid growth.

Federal Express displays many high involvement features. During the late 1980s, it began a company-wide push to convert to team working, including in the back office. It organized its 1,000 clerical workers in Memphis into super-teams of five to ten people and gave them the authority and training to manage themselves. These teams helped the company cut customer service problems, such as incorrect bills and lost packages, by 13 percent in 1989.

Whether one agrees that all three levels warrant the term 'empowerment', it is vital to distinguish between them to understand what the term can mean. It is equally important to know which form suits different situations. Bowen and Lawler make the point that there is no single approach which is ideal in every industry, company, function or situation. Like so many other things in management, the ideal degree and form of empowerment is contingent upon circumstances.

Common misinterpretations of empowerment

Empowerment is not:

1. **Delegation**. Management writer David Oates draws a distinction between delegation and empowerment: 'Delegation,' he says, 'is actioned by the manager. Empowerment, if it works well, is actioned by the subordinate.'[9]

   Jack Furrer, director of management education at the Swiss pharmaceutical multinational Ciba-Geigy, agrees: 'All too often, delegation equals dumping. Sometimes it's more positive and consists of a balance between direction and autonomy. But it still usually lacks the element of support which empowerment involves.'[10]

2. **Responsibility.** Responsibility alone is not empowerment, says Paul Evans, a professor of organizational behaviour at the French business school INSEAD. 'Empowerment is not just a matter of pushing more responsibility down an

organization,' he says. 'It's stupid and crazy to do so to people who don't have the skills and competencies to take control over their work.'

As Firestone CEO John Nevin puts it: 'If you want to drive a person crazy, the easiest way to do it is to give him a deep sense of responsibility and no authority.'[11]

INSEAD's Evans, however, prefers the French term *responsabilization* to empowerment. The latter, he says, 'constitutes the worst of Americanese. If one has to use a term, then I would prefer the French word, which is less emotive and misleading.'

3. **A cost-cutting exercise.** 'Are people being empowered to develop the business or are they being asked to cut costs and bring in short term profits?' asks Bernard Taylor of Henley Management College. 'People aren't fools,' he says:

> They need some vision of the future and some reassurance that the job will still be there in a few years. This requires some commitment to develop the business. At the moment, however, companies have got a major problem in motivating their employees and persuading them to commit themselves. This has come about because the unions have been disempowered, a massive amount of restructuring has led to large job losses, companies are traded like commodities, and managers and employees do not know from one minute to the next if they have a job. Empowerment is often introduced in the context of a siege mentality.

WHY IS EMPOWERMENT IMPORTANT NOW?

Though the word 'empowerment' in a management context has been coined relatively recently, its roots in management theory reach back several decades. The Hawthorne experiment at Westinghouse, where it was shown that productivity improved when staff felt they were being paid attention to, dates back to the 1920s. After the Second World War, the occupying forces installed works directors in major German companies, but baulked at the idea of taking the same medicine at home.

It wasn't until the 1960s, and the understandable backlash to the time and motion approach popular in the previous decade, that the idea of greater job involvement really came to the fore. It was at this point that a number of management scientists, notably Smith and McGregor, Drucker and Likert, began to question the role of people in the new, highly auto-mated workplace. This led to the concept of job enrichment – that, while repetitive motions may be the most technically efficient way of doing a job, a more varied job role could lead to greater motivation and productivity.

In Scandinavia during the 1960s and 1970s the free-thinking Einar Thorsrud and his colleagues at the Arbeidspsykologisk Institute in Oslo encouraged companies to experiment with semi-autonomous work groups. In the 1970s, technical advances in machine tools made it possible to pro-mote concepts such as group technology, where production was focused on 'cells' where large tasks were undertaken by multiskilled operators. At the same time, a handful of radical European entrepreneurs, such as the German Hauni, gave employees the right to select their own managers and, eventu-ally, ownership of their own enterprises.

Quality circles, imported from Japan, opened Western eyes to the potential contribution people at operator level can make, and the popularity of Total Quality Management added to the impetus.

Empowerment, in all its forms, evolved slowly from all these ideas. In the late 1980s, however, trends in the busi-ness world began to make it essential to delegate more wide-ly and to delegate more worthwhile work. The need has arisen to:

❑ make organizations more responsive to the market-place

❑ de-layer organizations in order to make them more responsive and cost effective

❑ get employees of various disciplines to collaborate with minimal supervision, by communicating horizontally, rather than vertically up and down the hierarchy

❑ get CEOs and top management to step back and do more strategic work

❑ tap all resources that can help maintain and improve competitiveness

❑ fulfil the higher expectations of an increasingly well-educated workforce.

Michael Osbaldeston, chief executive of Ashridge Management College, told a 1993 conference audience why he thinks empowerment has become so important in recent years:

❑ The increasing pace of change, the turbulence of the environment, the speed of competitive response and the acceleration of customer demands require a speed and flexibility of response which is incompatible with the old-style command and control model of organizational functioning.

❑ Organizations themselves are changing. The impact of downsizing, de-layering and decentralizing means that the old methods of achieving coordination and control are no longer appropriate. Achieving performance in these new circumstances requires that staff take and exercise much greater responsibility.

❑ Organizations require more cross-functional working, more cooperation between areas, more integration in their processes if they are to meet customers' needs. Such cooperation can be achieved through empowerment.

❑ Really good managerial talent is increasingly perceived as scarce and expensive. Using it for direct supervision of staff able to manage themselves compounds these difficulties. Empowerment, on the other hand, enables managerial talent to be focused more on external challenges and less on internal problem-solving.

❑ Empowerment may reveal sources of managerial talent, which were previously unrecognized, creating circumstances in which that talent can flourish.

❑ Staff are no longer prepared to accept the old command and control systems. Much wider availability of education, greater emphasis on lifetime development, and the end of the previous certainties of job security and steady advancement have contributed to a situation where jobs are valued for the development opportunities that they offer, rather than in themselves. Organizations which fail to meet these aspirations will not generate the performance they require and will suffer a continuous haemorrhaging of their best staff.

Stephen Brandt, of the Stanford Business School, gives a useful history lesson:

A hundred years ago, businesses – at least manufacturers – were dependent on craftsmen. The personal skills and commitment of people, the employees, were central to the success of a given enterprise. Early in this century, craft production gave way (grudgingly) to mass production – a new organizing philosophy for companies that made things. The result? The consumer got lower costs but at the expense of variety and by means of work methods that most employees found boring and dispiriting.

In short the essence of managing in those times was to plan, organize, lead and control so that most employees could leave their brains parked at the door as they entered the workplace. Is that era behind us? The answer seems to be 'yes' as financial results and market shares shift to favour companies in which employees bring their brains to work every day.[12]

Paul Neate, director of operations strategic development at Rothmans International, says:

People who go into our factories and offices manage what is in effect a very dynamic business in their domestic lives. They budget their household expenditure. They borrow money in huge amounts and service loans against a background of unpredictable fluctuations in interest rates. They have children who they strive to educate, often at great personal sacrifice. They carry out repairs to buildings and to vehicles; they are members of clubs, often holding office on committees dealing with substantial sums of money. And yet, when they come to our factories, we not only often give them simple and meaningless tasks but, as added insult, we appoint someone to overlook them. In these circumstances it is hardly surprising that their overlooker becomes demotivated and petty, while the overlooked becomes resentful and contemptuous of the organization that so treats him.[13]

Arthur Catteral, a consultant with the Coverdale Organisation, agrees:

> If you listen to commuters coming home on the trains you will hear many of them talking intensely to colleagues or friends about their jobs. Much of the time they are griping about another colleague or their boss. If you eavesdropped for five minutes you would soon realize that what they were complaining about was a lack of power in their everyday work situation.

Catteral once heard a hospital employee bitterly complaining that the company was no longer paying for the staff Christmas meal. She said that she didn't want to go anyway. To her, a job was something you did for money and then went home. But, Catteral says,

> someone who cared that much to spend her free time discussing the issue so fervently patently did care about her job and it did mean more to her than a source of income. What empowerment should attempt to do is harness the energy that is spent moaning about a situation and channelling it into making the job better. People do have a fundamental interest in their own jobs.

Empowered companies have also seen, or hope to see, a number of the following measurable benefits from empowering their staff.

Quality

'Most companies feel that they need to have constant improvement in order to be competitive,' says William Byham, author of *Zapp! the Lightning of Empowerment*.

> Well, how do you get people to improve constantly? I feel strongly that the only way you can do that is to get people to own their jobs. You can't talk them into it, you can't control them into it, and you can't compensate them into it. None of those things work in the long term. What empowerment does is to give them the motivation to improve.[14]

TQM demands a high level of commitment to problem recognition and resolution at all three levels – individual, team and organizational. The teams involved are often from several functions, so have little natural group loyalty or group commitment. The only way to generate group loyalty rapidly is for the teams to feel that they have the power not only to recommend significant changes, but to ensure that such changes come about.

Innovation

Another important aspect of empowerment is that it releases people's creativity and commitment. Indeed, many companies perceive this as the primary corporate objective of empowerment programmes. This may also be why these programmes so often fail, for the other side of the equation – the cost of persuading employees to give their creativity and commitment freely – is the genuine transfer of power and influence, and that is often too high a price to pay.

Staff loyalty and retention

According to a Confederation of British Industry report,

> there is a compelling logic in favour of effective employee involvement. It is not simply that the principle of employers involving and consulting their employees about matters that affect them wins widespread endorsement. Employers recognize that involvement makes good business sense.
> Regular provision of relevant information to employees, coupled with consultation on management proposals on these matters, fosters a shared commitment to the objectives of an organization. This in turn supports a positive climate in which employees are motivated to contribute to business success – with benefits for employers and employees alike.[15]

A feeling of powerlessness clearly decreases loyalty to an organization. However, the evidence for the extent to which empowerment increases loyalty is less clear. Logic suggests it should be so, but individual motivations will often distort the impact that empowerment has on people's feelings towards their employer.

There seems, however, to be solid evidence that labour turnover is higher in unempowered jobs than in empowered. A 1992 survey conducted by *Industry Week* magazine and the Association for Quality and Participation estimates that about 25 per cent of US companies have implemented empowerment somewhere within their organizations. These organizations – which range from manufacturers such as Texas Instruments and Digital Equipment Corporation to service companies such as Aid Association to Lutherans – have often achieved impressive results. They have substantially reduced labour turnover and improved productivity and service by 50 per cent or more. People stay in jobs they enjoy.[16]

Not everyone stays in empowered jobs, however. At Harvester Restaurants staff turnover actually rose in the first six months after empowerment was brought in in 1992. The disruption, increased responsibility and new way of working did not suit everyone.

Educated people, in particular, are increasingly using the amount of discretionary power available to them as a factor in choosing employers, and people will place less emphasis on salary and working conditions if they gain strong personal fulfilment from their work. In a 1991 Gallup poll, US workers were asked what they valued most in a job. With a 64 per cent response, 'ability to work independently' beat even 'high income' and 'chances for promotion'.

One area where empowerment may have a strong relationship to loyalty is in middle management, where whole layers of jobs have disappeared as Western companies have sought to reduce bureaucracy and cut costs. Flattening the management hierarchy reduces prospects of promotion and has made many remaining managers question the company's commitment to them and their commitment to the company. Empowerment is increasingly seen as a tool to renew that commitment.

Productivity and profit

'One of the major reasons for decline in American industrial productivity is the failure of corporate managers to manage resources effectively,' argue Barry and Irving Bluestone, a political economist and a professor of labour studies, respectively.

> That productivity growth has been lost in the labour intensive service sector, suggests that how labour is used in the firm may well be a dominant reason for the collapse in US productivity growth. A study of corporate efficiency conducted by Theodore H Barry Associates, a management consulting firm, found that only 4.4 hours of a typical American employee's work day are used productively. This research does not necessarily imply that labour is lazy in America. Rather, it suggests that workers are poorly managed, that their intelligence, skill and motivation go underused.[17]

The Bluestones cite the work of Harvard professor Quinn Mills, who claims that companies he has studied, which have successfully empowered their employees, often achieve productivity gains of 30–50 per cent year on year.

They also point to McDonelly Corporation, a Michigan-based manufacturer of mirrors and glass products, where worker self-management is credited with improving productivity between 1975 and 1984 by 110 per cent, a compounded rate of better than 7 per cent a year, or five times greater than the national average. 'Despite the grave recession that struck the auto industry in the early 90s, the company continued to expand and remain profitable. The company openly credits its success to employee empowerment.'

A recent measure of productivity at the British finance company, Frizzell Financial Services, showed a 62 per cent gain. Training manager Tony Miller claimed well over £250,000 in savings resulting from empowerment. Although some of these savings are arguably associated with the general re-engineering of the company, others can be directly attributed to people taking increased responsibility. Frizzell's divisional director Ian Wooley said: 'Empowerment has definitely saved 18 jobs. Localized problem solving has saved £198,000. There has also been a drop in sickness absence, an increase in calls handled and a rise in total sales, some of which is put down to empowerment.' However, it should be pointed out that Frizzell was undergoing a rapid expansion anyway.[18]

The learning organization

A learning organization is one which helps individuals develop an appetite for beneficial change, in terms of behaviour and skills that stick. Empowerment is not only a tool that can help bring about the learning organization, it is a necessary part of a learning organization. If individuals do not have the freedom to improve the situation in which they find themselves to common purpose, then you do not have a learning organization in place.

Empowered employees often have to take over roles which are traditionally not within their job description – for example training others, advising more senior people, holding seminars, and even research and development. The only way they can cope with these added demands is if they work in an organization that allows them to develop continually and helps them to keep abreast of the needs of their job by giving them access to learning tools. These tools can range from links with universities, to training seminars and open learning centres.

Peter Senge in his book *The Fifth Discipline* gives four factors that provide a vital dimension to building organizations that can learn, that can continually enhance their capacity to realize their highest aspirations:[19]

1. **personal mastery:** organizations can learn only through individuals who learn.

2. **Mental models:** unexamined assumptions, especially in the minds of key decision-makers, limit an organization's range of actions to what is familiar and comfortable. Questioning the status quo and received wisdom is essential to learning.

3. **Building a shared vision:** Senge believes people seek to build shared visions because they desire to be connected in an important undertaking. Shared vision is vital for the learning organization because it provides the focus and energy for learning.

4. **Team learning:** the process of aligning and developing the capacity of a team to create the results its members truly desire.

The concept of the learning organization has much in common with those of total quality management and empowerment. All three are based on the idea of continuous improvement; all have a strong emphasis on feedback, creativity, teamwork and problem solving. These concepts can only be truly successful if they operate alongside each other.

Survival

To all of these reasons there is one, overriding imperative – survival! Organizations that intend to compete cannot implement the continuous changes required by a competitive environment without the goodwill, commitment and understanding of the vast majority of both managers and employees. It is possible to galvanize a workforce into accepting change when the crisis is big and real enough and the stick long and hard enough. But the edge of fear wears off. The crisis motivation too easily degenerates into deep resignation. To maintain the pace of change it is necessary to move people from acceptance to embracing opportunities. Such a movement – especially when the changes proposed involve a degree of pain – can only come about when people feel they understand what is going on and why; when they feel in at least partial control of what happens to and around them and feel supported by peers and by the organization itself. One way of describing those feelings is empowerment.

One large retailer, in a crisis situation, tried, and failed, to introduce an empowerment programme into its stores. The company, in a turnaround situation, needed to show significant improvements in sales as quickly as possible. Management trained shop and warehouse staff at each site de-layered the management structure and encouraged frontline people to take on supervisory responsibilities. It worked remarkably well at first – sales turnover went up by 20 per cent and more. But:

❑   it was costly, both in training expenses and in learning by making mistakes

❑   no one ever talked to the staff about the outcomes, or
about what was in it for them.

When the time came to move to the next phase, where staff
were to take on even more responsibility, the union, which
had been passive so far, reacted badly. 'Where's our pay-
off?', the union wanted to know. Management was taken
completely by surprise.

WHAT'S IN IT FOR EMPLOYEES?

The above example illustrates a critical, if often overlooked
point about empowerment: many employees are not prepared to take on more work and responsibility simply for the
pleasure of feeling more in control. Too many empowerment
programmes are presented as a devolution of power, responsibility – and work – from management to staff, with little
thought about what is really in it for the people at the sharp
end.
   Staff, when the issues have not been communicated to
them properly, understandably resent what they see as simply 'getting them to do the manager's job.' This is not to say
that staff need to be compensated financially for being
empowered. Patently what is usually not in it for employees
is extra pay or automatic promotions. Though many empowered employees *are* financially better off, because of profit-
sharing or employee ownership plans, empowered employees
are not, as a rule, paid for the extra responsibility they take
on. Even Ricardo Semler, CEO of Semco Brazil, which is
looked upon by managers the world over as a thriving example of empowerment, drives as hard a bargain as any industrial chief at pay negotiation time. Promotions are even less
likely to occur in empowered organizations than in unempowered ones, because of their flat structure. When
Harvester Restaurants introduced empowerment, the first
taste many staff got of it was a demotion. Assistant managers
became team leaders and waiters, albeit very responsible
ones, because their job stratum had disappeared. Few people
minded though, because empowerment can be a powerful

motivation in itself, provided it is handled and communicated effectively.

Here is how some employees we spoke to reacted to the way empowerment has changed their jobs.

For Hazel Mayo, a packaging operator at Walkers Smiths Snack Foods Lincoln factory, it has meant that

> people on the line have a chance to get a lot more involved. We all have more responsibility for the job now. It's not a case of 'that's my job, this is yours'. Now we are all involved in making the product. Now, for instance, packers have the power to say: 'this product isn't good enough, I'm not packing it.'

'I take the projects I work on very personally now. I feel if the projects don't succeed, I haven't succeeded, so I'll move mountains to make sure they work,' says Andrew Tyler, a marine scientist at British Marine Technology.

Ocelia Williams, a line employee Cine Made Inc. in Cincinnati, takes a pragmatic view of the changes at her workplace: 'I like my job more than I ever used to. I do better work. I make more money. I suppose [owner] Bob Frey is getting rich on those same profits, but that's life. He has more invested in this company than I do. And that's fine.'[20]

Nuruz Zaman, an inspector with the Indian Agricultural Extension Service in Assam, says: 'Since doing the [team-working and empowerment skills] course, I've tried things out in the villages that I never would have tried before. I have greater clarity about what I want to achieve and more careful planning has already saved me some 10 to 20 per cent of time.'

Empowerment can, however, be a double-edged blade for many people, as Pat Winter, a personal assistant at one of Berkshire County Council's district offices, discovered. For several years, Winter had been responsible only for basic secretarial duties. After the council devolved many of its functions to the districts, she was put in charge of monitoring her district's finances and checking that the district was staying within budget. To do this, she had to master a number of computer skills and accounting techniques she had never had to deal with before:

Because I mastered the computer and a lot of staff here have difficulty with it at first, I also teach those who are having problems with it. This saves money for the council and gives me a chance to meet other people in the organization. Before the changes, this would not have been possible.

There are, however, drawbacks to her new job, she adds:

I enjoyed my job before, but now I have much more responsibility. It is a lot harder and, although I have got a kick out of learning these new skills, the work has encroached on my home life at times. With three children this can create a clash of priorities. Also I don't get any more money for this increased responsibility.

CONCLUSION

Empowerment, difficult as it is to define, is a process that virtually every organization must at least consider if it is to remain competitive. Considering it is one thing – making it a reality is another. In the next chapter, we will look at options for implementing empowerment in various types of organizations.

References

1. Kizilos, P., 'Crazy about empowerment', *Training*, December 1990.

2. Oates, D., *Leadership: The Art of Delegation,* Century Business Books: London, 1993.

3. *Employee Commitment and the Skills Revolution,* The Policy Studies Institute, June 1993. (Part of the Employment in Britain Survey.)

4. 'Empowerment, a leap of faith?', *Management Training*, August 1993.

5. Pfeffer, J., 'Power: The not-so-dirty secret to success in organizations', *Stanford Business School Magazine*, March 1992.

6. Stewart, T.A., 'A user's guide to power', *Fortune*, 6 November 1989.

7. Stewart, ibid.

8. Bowen, D.E. and Lawler, E.E., 'The empowerment of service workers: what, why, how and when', *Sloan Management Review*, Spring 1992, Volume 33, No. 3.

9. Oates, D., *Leadership*, op. cit.

10. Lorenz, C., 'Power to the people', *Financial Times*, 30 March 1992.

11. Stewart, T.A., 'A user's guide to power', op. cit.

12. Brandt, S.C., 'Bring your brains to work please', *Stanford Business School Magazine*, December 1991.

13. Neate, P., Speaking at an IIR seminar, November 1992.

14. Kizilos, P, 'Crazy about empowerment', op. cit.

15. *Social Europe After Maastricht, Freedom Not License*, Confederation of British Industry, March 1992

16. Wellins, R., 'Building self-directed teams', *Technical and Skills Training*, May/June 1992.

17. Bluestone, B. and Bluestone, I., 'Workers (and managers) of the world unite', *Technology Review*, November/December 1992.

18. Pickard, J., 'The real meaning of empowerment', *Personnel Management*, November 1993.

19. Senge, P., *The Fifth Discipline*, Century Business: London, 1990.

20. Frey, R., 'Empowerment or else', *Harvard Business Review*, September–October 1993.

2
PRACTICAL STARTING POINTS

There is nothing more difficult to carry out, nor more doubtful of success,
nor more dangerous to handle, than to initiate a new order of things.

Nicholo Machiavelli

Empowerment is about being free to explore the best way of doing things
– not just doing what you are told.

Richard Carver, managing director of the Coverdale Organisation

Where there is no vision, the people perish.

Proverbs 29.18

Defining empowerment may be an interesting enough exercise; but in reality, arguing about the definition of empowerment doesn't contribute very much to the job of making it work. In this chapter we look at how to go about conceiving and planning an empowerment programme, based mainly on observation of what helps and hinders empowerment initiatives – whatever they may be called.

The first rule is that there are no rules. What works and what doesn't in putting empowerment into practice is as varied as the organizations attempting to implement it. However, while it is impractical to be prescriptive at this stage, it is possible to highlight some general principles that do seem to apply in all the cases we have encountered:

First define your purpose

An important aspect of empowerment is clarity of purpose – a change team must first define what it wants empowerment to accomplish, before it can decide how to implement it. Says

Coverdale's Richard Carver:

> Unless an organization and the individuals within it are clear about the purpose that lies behind a task, they can't possibly take effective decisions about how to do it. The same task with a different purpose would be done in entirely different ways.
>
> The level of empowerment that suits a given organization depends on the extent to which it is helpful to have individuals free to improve their situation. Empowerment in the armed services, for example, might be a very different kettle of fish than empowerment in a process consultancy. There may, however, be more common ground than we think – the boundaries have yet to be pushed really severely. There is an element of any job in which discretion and the freedom to improve the way it is done is helpful.

Consultant Wally Cork agrees: 'What we are really looking for is effective behaviours; and clearly, which is the most effective will depend on the situation. Sometimes, in the midst of an emergency for example, autocratic behaviour is the best way to get things done.'

American business academics David Bowen and Edward Lawler suggest five contingencies that can help determine what level of empowerment to adopt:

1. **Type of business strategy**: a production line approach makes the most sense if your core mission is to offer high-volume service at the lowest cost. The production line approach does not rule out suggestion involvement. Employees often have ideas even when much of their work is routine.

2. **Tie to the customer**: empowerment is best when the service delivery involves managing a relationship, as opposed to simply performing a transaction. The returns are higher with more sophisticated services and delivery systems. The more intangible the service and the more enduring the relationship, the stronger the case for empowerment.

3. **Technology**: in some cases, such as fast food production or telephone exchanges, the design of the technology limits the possibility for empowerment. When technology constrains empowerment, service managers can still sup-

port front-line employees in ways that enhance their satisfaction and the service quality they provide. Routine work can be engaging if employees are convinced that it matters. For example, volunteers can happily spend hours licking envelopes in a fund-raising campaign for their favourite charity.

4. **Business environment:** businesses that operate in unpredictable environments benefit more than most from empowerment. In airlines, for example, it is impossible to anticipate many of the situations that will arise and programme employees to respond to them. Employees trained in purposeful chaos are appropriate for unpredictable environments.

5. **Types of employees:** for empowerment to work, the company needs to have managers who believe that their employees can act independently. If managers believe that employees must be closely supervised, then the production line approach may be the only feasible option. Employees will respond positively to empowerment only if they have strong needs to grow and to deepen and test their abilities at work. Some employees simply prefer a production line approach.

Define what empowerment means for your organization – and communicate it

'Empowerment can be a dangerous word to use,' says consultant Arthur Catterall. 'Many companies use the word without qualifying it; but, if a company is to undertake an empowerment programme it is vital that the managers ensure there is a clear definition of what it will mean. If they don't define clear parameters on empowerment, people may feel cheated.'

In one organization Catterall worked with, for example, staff were told they were empowered, but were left to decide for themselves what that meant. So, when decisions were then made at senior level without consultation with the workforce, people who thought they were empowered felt surprised and disempowered. The management team in turn were surprised that their people had thought they could make such policy decisions.

To avoid such misunderstandings, says Catterall,

a company moving towards empowerment should first canvass its employees on the nature of the empowerment and their views on how it should happen. It is important to find out how people feel about the way things are and how they would like them to be before they start.

Be prepared to make substantial changes in behaviours and systems at three levels: organization, team and individual

Empowerment programmes often fail because organizations fail to grasp this concept and focus empowerment efforts on only one or two levels, usually the lowest.

The more people are involved, the more difficult it is to achieve. Managers can always empower the occasional individual who is an obvious self-starter, of sufficient initiative, professionalism and natural judgement that it requires only a small act of faith to hand over tasks in their entirety. Similarly, the individual, who has been a good number two for a long time, frequently earns the empowerment that comes with familiarity.[1]

At a team level, however, the relationship between the manager and the individual team members will vary considerably, as will the capacity of each team member to operate independently. Power needs to be disseminated, rather than focused. It should be contained within the team as a whole and moved between the members according to need. Managers need to move out of the team structure in order for people to use the power they have rather than constantly refer up for decisions.

At an organizational level, empowerment is essentially a philosophy, rather than a practical tool of management. If most of the power has been distributed among teams, the role of management becomes one of making sure things get done through influence and support.

Decide what degree of discretion best suits your purpose

Bowen and Lawler draw an interesting comparison between Federal Express and the United Parcel Service (UPS) – two very successful businesses competing in the same industry, with a broadly similar service. The difference is that one offers staff a great deal of discretion, while the other opts for command and control.

> Federal Express is the first service organization to win the Malcolm Baldrige National Quality Award. The company's motto is 'People, service and profits'. Behind its blue, white and red planes and uniforms are self managing work teams, gainsharing plans, and empowered employees seemingly consumed with providing flexible and creative service to customers with varying needs.
>
> At UPS, referred to as Big Brown by its employees, the philosophy was stated by founder Jim Case: 'Best service at low rates'. Here too we find turned-on people and profits. But we do not find empowerment. Instead we find controls, rules, a detailed union contract, and carefully studied work methods. Nor do we find a promise to do all things for customers, such as handling off-schedule pick-ups and packages that don't fit size and weight limitations. In fact, rigid operational guidelines help guarantee the customer reliable, low cost service.
>
> Federal Express is a high involvement, horizontally coordinated organization that encourages employees to use their judgement above and beyond the rule book. UPS is a top-down traditionally controlled organization, in which employees are directed by policies and procedures based on industrial engineering studies of how all service delivery aspects should be carried out and how long they should take.

Bowen and Lawler also compare Disney Theme Parks, where ride operators are thoroughly scripted on what to say to guests with Club Med, where the resort's congenial hosts are set free to spontaneously create a holiday experience for their guests. Which is the better approach, Fed Ex or UPS, Club Med or Disney? Clearly, the success of all four companies shows that there is no firm answer to that.

The degree to which individuals and teams are able to take responsibility depends on several factors:

The scope of their knowledge and skills base

If people don't think they have the skills to do a job, they will normally be hesitant to take it on, if only for fear of failure. Part of the role of the manager is to imbue people with a can-do attitude, while enabling them to develop the necessary skills in a step-by-step manner. A key is to let people try short bursts of different activities.

Expanding people's knowledge base is a matter of enabling them to use their skills and common sense more efficiently, because they understand the context of the task more clearly. In a retail environment, for example, it may also be a matter of extending people's product knowledge. It can also be important to ensure that they have access to information that is relevant to their task, but which is held elsewhere.

The scope of discretion they have over what tasks are done

Usually, there is little opportunity for managers, let alone first-level staff, to decide which tasks should be done. A contract is made with a customer and this tends to provide a *fait accompli*. But there is always some room to manoeuvre. Some work teams now become involved in make-or-buy decisions on elements of projects – given sufficient costing information, they can decide for themselves which tasks should best be performed within the team and which can be parcelled out to subcontractors. Some years ago we even encountered a software company where staff bid for projects in a weekly auction!

The scope of discretion they have over when tasks are done

With clear, relatively simple processes and a precise definition of when the customer (internal or external) needs their output, first-level employees can often be entrusted with prioritizing their own work, either as individuals or as teams. Even within complex assembly operations, with computer-based workflow planning systems, it is possible to achieve greater efficiency by restricting the centrally scheduled activities to those which are essential for maintaining workflow, and delegating decisions on the rest to the workgroups themselves. A critical component here is clear guidelines about how to make priority decisions and an understanding of the broad assumptions that the logistics planners are making about priorities at a higher level.

The scope of discretion they have over how tasks are done

There is a hierarchy of discretion, as follows:

1. **Fully prescriptive.** A method study organization, for example, defines what actions an operator will perform, in what order, and often sets standard times for each action. Similarly, telesales people are sometimes given a word-for-word script, complete with when to pause. In both these examples, the emphasis is on control during the task. Operators may only break the procedures with permission from the manager.

2. **Guided prescriptive**. The process is mapped out into a mixture of fully prescriptive elements and elements where a limited amount of discretion is permitted. For example, in administering medicines, nurses have to follow very strict procedures. However, there is significant scope for discretionary behaviour in how they reassure the patient, which patients they spend most time with, and so on.

   Here the emphasis is on control of the critical elements of the task.

3. **Regulated**. There may be several valid ways of undertaking the task. While none of these is prescribed, there nonetheless exists a body of rules to define some actions as obligatory and to prohibit others. Guidance as to best practice may also assume the force of rules in this environment. For example, a book-keeping practice is constrained by rules from government, professional bodies and in-house custom.

   Here the emphasis is divided roughly equally between the outcomes and process control.

4. **Guided**. A process outline, which may have been agreed between the manager and the people doing the work, or even originated by the latter, is used as a template. For example, a telesales operator is permitted to use the role script as a general guide, but to develop a patter that best fits his or her personality and allows a more flexible response to different types of customer. Here, the emphasis of control shifts towards outputs rather than process.

5. **Goal-focused**. How the individual (or team) does the work is irrelevant, as long as it fulfils two sets of key criteria. These are:

   — goals: what has to be done, by when, and the budgetary/resource constraints
   — co-dependency: an obligation to consider and manage the impact upon other people of how the task is done. For example, when a production team in a bespoke publishing operation may find it a chore to complete timesheets, but failure to do so would make it impossible for the accounts department to issue correct invoices.

   The more responsibilities a team can take upon itself, the fewer co-dependency constraints it will encounter. For example, when the publishing production team has responsibility for its own billing, it automatically records time spent, because the team members can see the immediate effect on their budgets.

6. **Capability-focused or self-defining**. These are relatively rare, but there are work teams which define both what they do and how they do it, within their own frames of reference. For example, some insolvency practitioners operate in teams with a very broad brief. They typically decide which cases to take on, what objectives should be set in each case, and how they will achieve them.

   Such individuals or teams have substantial freedom, because there is no pre-existing organizational structure to constrain them and often no customer with sufficient power to insist upon closely defined project objectives. Such teams also tend to be driven by the capability and ambitions of their members, rather than by an external definition of task.

Even within their own organizations, these professionals usually have the freedom to operate that comes from partner status. As long as activities fall broadly within the recognized arena of the profession, do not become a financial drain on the organization, and meet legal requirements, they are condoned or encouraged.

Within large organizations, teams with similar behaviours can evolve as a response to major change. Usually *ad hoc*, with a very broad remit to design and drive through a change initiative, they tend to cut across functional boundaries, reporting directly to the chief executive. The power these teams assume is partly delegated by the CEO, but typically also evolves by virtue of the energy the team exhibits and the initial successes it achieves.

The degree to which an organization, or a part of one, can tolerate discretionary power depends on a number of factors, including the importance of process control. The diagram below provides a useful means of identifying the relative importance of process control versus individual or team outcomes in an organization.

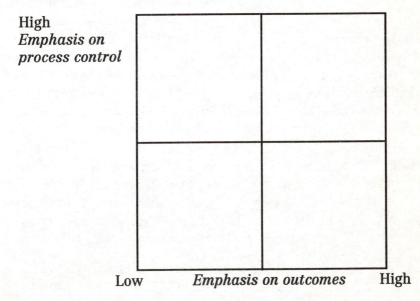

High
*Emphasis on
process control*

Low   *Emphasis on outcomes*   High

Organizations with low emphasis on individual or team outcomes and high emphasis on process control leave very little room for discretionary decision-making. For example, at some fast food chains, even the smile is scripted into the customer encounter. Similarly, many retail chains believe that consistency of pricing, presentation and stock range is more important than local initiative, and is an important part of the customer promise.

Organizations with high emphasis on outcomes but low emphasis on process controls typically set people targets and let them decide for themselves how to achieve them. Success is well rewarded; failure frequently means parting company. This approach is typical of many sales operations, but its weakness is that the individuals or teams may feel unsupported, while opportunities for building best practice into procedures across the organization are frequently lost.

Organizations with high emphasis on both process controls and outcomes can become schizophrenic. It is possible to set tough targets and to be very prescriptive about how people achieve them, but the likelihood is that creativity of response will be a casualty of this dual emphasis.

The resolution to the problem appears to be in part to emphasize processes not process controls. In other words, to sell the value of processes to people, so they adopt them. In a study in the early 1980s, David Clutterbuck compared the attitudes of managers towards very similar sets of business controls. Managers in the most successful companies thought that the controls were there to help them. Managers in the less successful companies often perceived the same control systems to be there for the benefit of someone else.

Organizations which have low emphasis on both process control and outputs are unlikely to be high performers. They may typically be state-run monopolies. Under privatization or other similar upheavals, top management will try to move them to one of the other three boxes – often, incongruously, to the high process control/high output orientation box – an exceptionally difficult, if not impossible, transition to manage.

The degree to which they are able to influence policy

Policies are usually established at business level, for a number of good practical reasons. Empowered organizations attempt to reduce to a minimum the volume of central policy-making.

In making decisions as to where to allocate policy-making, the following check list can be helpful:

❑ Where is the impact of the policy felt most strongly?

❑ Who takes responsibility for the policy? (ie who is accountable for its success or failure?).

❑ Who needs to be consulted if the policy is to work?

❑ What is the lowest level to which policy-making on this issue could be delegated without causing serious problems? For example, IBM UK delegates are responsible for deciding the allocation of charitable contributions to the local level. John Lewis has the same policy.

❑ Is the policy aimed at constraining action or stimulating it?

A relevant issue here is breadth and detail of policy. Considerable freedom can be given to business units, for example, within a corporate charities policy that specifies only budget, the broad areas where the company wishes to see community investment made, and some general guidelines on how to select worthwhile, viable projects.

Even though the policy may be decided at business level, the ability to *influence* can be extended to all levels of the organization through:

❑ participation in cross-functional, cross-level panels to discuss and review policy

❑ opinion surveys

❑ open discussion of policy issues in company newspapers, team briefings and so on.

The opportunity to change systems that affect people in other departments or functions

One of the traditional tasks of middle and senior management has been to mediate between the competing needs of internal teams. A small change that would make life easier for people in the warehouse, for example, might create havoc for someone in the assembly operation. Sales frequently wishes to operate on a totally different set of lead times to those that production is prepared to concede. If these are considered *political* decisions, then they inevitably become the responsibility of someone fairly senior. If they are regarded as *logistics* decisions, to be decided in the best interests of the customer and of the overall cost to the company, they can much more readily be dealt with by the parties themselves.

Empowering companies aim to depoliticize cross-functional issues by creating opportunities for people to manage their own interfaces with other teams and functions.

Table 1 shows how various techniques can be used to implement different elements of empowerment.

Table I Techniques for empowerment

Some techniques for empowering

	Manual workers	Clerical workers	Professional workers
Scope of knowledge-base	• Job rotation • Group technology/ self-governing teams	• Job rotation • Self-governing teams • Job enlargement	• Job enlargement *and* • Narrowing focus to allow people to become experts
Scope of discretion over - when tasks are done - how tasks are done - design of new tasks - interpretation of policy	• Self-governing teams • Problem-solving skills • Delegation	• Self-governing teams • Problem-solving skills • Delegation	• Self-governing teams • Problem-solving skills • Delegation
Involvement in policy-making	• Referenda • Cascade briefings (with an emphasis on upward communications) • Participation (from consultative committees through employees on the board)		
Opportunity to change systems that affect people in other functions/departments	• Suggestion schemes • Cross functional quality improvement teams		

Retain an element of control for the purposes of quality, safety and service standards

Empowerment provides for a more efficient, cost-effective kind of control than command and control organizations, argues Jim Durcan, director of the leadership development programme at Ashridge Management College:

> There are two kinds of controls: controls that are imposed on the employee by the organization (external) and controls that are self-imposed (internal). The internal controls come from personal drives, such as pride in one's work, self-esteem and a sense of responsibility. External controls relate to the boss giving strict instructions governed by disciplinary procedures and penalties for poor performance.[2]

Durcan argues that internal controls are more effective and cheaper, because they don't tie up organizational resources.

At Harvester Restaurants, empowerment works because of an intensely tight overriding structure:

> The staff are empowered to do virtually anything except decide whether or not they will be empowered. The system [of team working roles] is all handed down and is the same for each restaurant. Only within that framework can they make their decisions. And they have tight targets to meet. For instance every waitress at the Dulwich restaurant is expected to sell a side order to every table. If they don't do this, the team will want to know what went wrong.[3]

Develp a common language

Says Richard Carver:

> For individuals to work with others in an empowered way, they need some sort of common language or way of approaching the work they do that accommodates different levels of expertise and different ways of thinking. This is a vital element of teamwork and, without this ingredient, those who are empowered can work effectively only on a solo basis.

Allow people to make mistakes

'If people are to be empowered, you can't expect them to take responsibility then feel insecure about their actions,' says Carver. 'You have to accept that sometimes employees will make mistakes.'

Don't expect a quick fix

Management writer Peter Kizilos also believes that too many companies are looking for an unrealistically easy route to empowerment, or at least the benefits of it:

> It's tempting to conclude that many companies are attracted by a fantasy version of empowerment and simultaneously repelled by the reality. How lovely to have energetic, dedicated workers who always seize the initiative (but only when 'appropriate') who enjoy taking risks (but never risky ones), who volunteer their ideas (but only brilliant ones), who solve problems on their own (but make no mistakes), who aren't afraid to speak their minds (but never ruffle any feathers), who always give their very best to the company (but ask no unpleasant questions about what the company is giving back). How nice it would be, in short, to empower workers without giving them any power.[4]

This kind of artificial empowerment can be worse than doing nothing at all, he adds:

> When an organization pays lip service to the ideals of empowerment but fails to nurture an environment that supports empowered behaviour, employees may become cynical, withdrawing further than ever from alignment with the company's goals. Mixed messages are another sure way to make employees suspicious and cynical about empowerment.

Author William Byham, one of the biggest beneficiaries of the trend towards empowerment, is himself concerned by the quick fix attitude many organizations have taken. Byham points out that a surprising number of companies are simply handing out his best-selling book to employees and calling that an empowerment programme: 'A whole lot of Zapp books went to companies who thought that all they had to do was give people the book. I'm not complaining about the number of copies we've sold, but I feel bad about it,' he confessed. Asked if it had just become a buzzword, Byham agreed: 'It's getting that way. One of the big problems is that companies are committing themselves to empowerment without knowing what it means, and therefore they are not getting anything out of it.'[5]

At the French business school INSEAD, Paul Evans has carried out informal research into the difference between successful and unsuccessful empowerment programmes, with some chilling results.

> The conclusion appears to be that the common denominator among the successes is that empowerment was only used as a post hoc label for what had happened; in all cases the organization changes were driven by some visible variant on the explicit business object of how to do things better, cheaper, and faster. This resulted in flatter, more horizontal organization and what was called afterwards empowerment. The common denominator among the failures was an explicit focus upon empowerment, so that means became ends, ultimately engendering misunderstanding and widespread frustration. The concept of empowerment, as it is often used, fosters this trap.

Another trap is the way, according to Lawler, that many of the organizational changes needed to put empowerment in place actually disempower people, at least in the short term. 'You cannot see empowerment as an issue on its own,' he says. 'It comes alongside restructuring, downsizing, the phasing out of large employee pressure groups and process re-engineering. Most of these processes tend to disempower people by robbing them of people, budget, or at worst, their job itself.'[6]

One large public sector organization fell into this trap. The CEO set up a change programme and gave a lot of power to the change management team – a multi-level, multi-disciplinary group brought together for the purpose. The senior management team gave this *ad hoc* team its blessing and commitment. However, the change team's activities were then put in the hands of the deputy CEO, leaving the top team feeling marginalized and disempowered. They sensed, quite rightly, that the centre of the organization had shifted away from them. Nothing was said at that point, but when the CEO departed and his deputy took his place, the top team's resentment came out in the form of blocking all the change team's recommendations. Their behaviour was a direct result of feeling disempowered, even though they themselves had set out to make the changes happen.

Another difficulty many companies encounter is what could be called the 'who goes first' syndrome. Many organizations reach an advanced stage in their empowerment process only to find the initiative loses steam. They have made most of the necessary structural changes, the management team is – in principle – prepared to release authority, and employees have come to expect to be consulted on issues affecting them, yet the final transfer of power eludes both staff and management. One factory manager in this situation told the authors: 'We want to empower people, but they have to prove to us that they are ready for it', while front-line employees at the same organization said: 'We could do so much more if managers would consult us and tell us what is expected of us.'

Lawler adds that if many organizations actually knew what they were getting into, they might not be so enthused:

> A lot of companies are not making the very substantial changes they need to make in their overall organization design and management practices. Only by making such changes can a company create real empowerment rather than temporary flurries of activity. It's a very long-term, hard process if you're talking about changing a major corporation. It involves at least eight to ten years of activity and changing just about every piece of the management systems.

Be prepared to take a step back from empowerment

'Unless there is a serious, long-term commitment to changing the organization's culture in radical ways, it may be better to walk away from the empowerment game,' says Lawler.

> Even if the change effort is done well, there are questions about whether this is the best way to manage in all situations. And if the effort is done poorly, there are enormous risks. If

you execute it poorly, you're probably worse off than if you execute a more traditional management style poorly because the chances for chaos are greater.

One company routinely cited as an empowering place to work is Hewlett Packard. Yet external pressures have taken a toll on even that vaunted corporate culture, according to Tony Coleman, a human resource development manager for HP's circuit technology group in Palo Alto, California. 'The fact of the matter is that we've lost some of that direction,' Coleman says.

> Competition is a lot more fierce, as well as a lot more global. It's really changed some of the fabric of the culture, not only in our company, but in others. The organization has been more directive in terms of getting things done. Newer employees are being told what to do rather than being given some broad objectives whereby they can select the methods and the means to get results.[7]

Empowerment at Frizzell Financial Services has not been without hiccups, either. When it was first introduced, there was a sense that, as divisional director Ian Wooley put it, 'the revolution had begun.'[8]

Supervisor Anne-Marie Griffiths says 'everyone came back from their training and thought: 'Right that's it; we're running the company.' 'In the first few weeks, everyone thought of themselves. They were going home early, having long lunch breaks and having a smoke when they wanted'. Darrin Vingoe, a coordinator for the team Griffiths supervises, adds: 'People would go for a cigarette and hope someone else would answer the phone. We weren't being totally irresponsible, but we were less productive.'

In fact, the teams were so unproductive that certain senior managers started to get cold feet and very nearly withdrew backing. But they were persuaded by the enthusiasts in the company to hold their ground and are now convinced this was the right decision.

Personnel manager David Tomlinson still doesn't like the term empowerment, though, describing it as just a buzzword. He views it as a 1990s form of job enrichment or employee involvement. 'We are going back to basic principles, trying to gain commitment from people by finding them a sense of ownership,' he says.

The experience of organizations like Hewlett Packard and Frizzell, which have managed to empower employees, suggests that it takes time and concentrated effort.

Among the lessons learned:

❑ People don't necessarily want to be empowered. The inevitable question: 'What's in it for me?' can be expected in any organization that suddenly tells people they are empowered. A major part of any empowerment campaign must be to help people persuade themselves of the benefits, to the customer, to the organization and to themselves.

❑ Empowering someone else is actually an impossibility. No one *has* to accept power. The most a manager can do is encourage them to do so. As Alistair Wright, human resource director at Digital Equipment, says: 'It took me a long time to learn a fundamental truth about empowerment: You cannot give empowerment. People themselves have to be in a position to want to do things.'[9]

❑ People can often take additional power only in small doses. After a lifetime of being told how to do the job and being prevented from using their initiative, they will naturally be cautious about accepting what might, for all they know, be a poisoned chalice.

❑ Consistency is essential. Managers at all levels have to learn not only to give up control of tasks, but to resist the temptation to seize back control when they don't agree with the decisions made.

❑ You can't simply adapt the rulebooks; you have to throw them away and start again. Very few activities require company-wide rules; most rules should be generated within the team, as a help to the team and as a means of ensuring the consistency of service processes. Those rules you do need can be divided into those that are strict (inviolable) and those that are standard (which should normally be observed, but which may be broken in exceptional cases, where there is a specific customer need). Virtually all other activities can be covered with broad guidance or left to the discretion of the employee.

WHAT DOES AN EMPOWERED ORGANIZATION LOOK LIKE?

According to management journalist Jay Finegan, companies with a high level of job autonomy usually have the following characteristics:[10]

❑ they invest a lot of time and effort in hiring, to make sure new recruits can handle workplace freedom

❑ their organizational hierarchy is flat

❑ they set loose guidelines, so workers know their decision-making parameters

❑ accountability is paramount – results matter more than process

❑ high quality performance is always expected

❑ openness and strong communication are encouraged

❑ employee satisfaction is a core value.

According to Richard Carver, empowered companies should reflect the following characteristics:

❑ everyone in the organization is valued and encouraged to make a personal contribution

❑ individuals are continually aware not only of what they are seeking to achieve, but also why they are seeking to achieve it and how it fits with the wider corporate goals

❑ the culture is likely to be cooperative and purposeful, rather than blame-oriented

❑ individuals have a real willingness to take personal responsibility for their own success, the success of the team in which they work and the organization as a whole.

Other signs of an organization where empowerment is likely

to flourish are listed in Table 2 below. But there are other, useful acid tests, among them that used by the Baldrige Award examiners. David Garvin, former CEO of Motorola, expressed it this way in a *Harvard Business Review* article:

> To see if empowerment really exists, examiners look at the ability of front-line employees to act in the interests of customers without getting prior approval. Can a saleswoman, on her own authority, make a $5000 adjustment for a customer, or is she limited to $10 or less? Can a customer service representative deviate from established procedures if he feels it will help a client, or must he clear it first with his boss? Within the factory, do employees have access to a 'stop the line' button that they can use to halt the assembly line if they detect quality problems? Because these steps are so much more effective when they are accompanied by a supportive environment, examiners probe further on supervisory practices. What happens when things go wrong? Are employees punished, or do they receive coaching and support? Is personal initiative valued or feared?

Consultant Wally Cork has a quicker acid test:

> You know you have an empowered organization when you, as the managing director, walk through the factory and are stopped by an operator who says, 'Hey Fred, I've spoken and written to all kinds of people about this problem and now I want to know what *you* are going to do about it.'

Table 2 The organization that empowers

From	To
Fear	Challenge and adventure
Learning is a chore	Learning is an adventure
Dependence	Mutual independence
People take little initiative	People solve their own problems
	People suggest solutions to other people's problems
	People have the skills to work without supervision
Scant training and development	Continuous development
Avoiding change	Continuous change welcomed
Feedback is seen as criticism	Feedback seen as essential
Past experience has no relevance	Pause, reflect and learn
Training and development is the responsibility of personnel	Training and development is everyone's responsibility

Lack of vision	Strong, focused and shared vision
Problem avoiding	Problem solving
Closed communications	Open communications
	- sharing of information
	- sharing of ideas
	- sharing of skills
Distrust and suspicion	Trust

CONCLUSION

It is essential, in introducing empowerment, to define first what it means to you. As Coverdale consultant Keith Edwards points out: 'Empowerment is one of these catch-all phrases which doesn't mean anything until the organization has spelt out what it really means.'

In this chapter we have looked at how to define what empowerment means to an individual organization and reviewed the range of empowerment options available – a range that is potentially as varied as organizations themselves.

In the next chapter we take a harder look at the nuts and bolts of empowerment – creating empowered structures.

References

1. Armistead, C., Clarke, G. and Clutterbuck, D. *Inspired Customer Service*, Kogan Page, London, 1993.

2. Cited in Oates, D., *Leadership: The Art of Delegation*, Century Business Books, London, 1993.

3. Pickard, J., 'The real meaning of empowerment', *Personnel Management*, November 1993.

4. Kizilos, P., 'Crazy about empowerment', *Training*, December 1990.

5. Pickard, J. 'The real meaning of empowerment', op. cit.

6. Quoted in Kizilos, P., 'Crazy about empowerment', op. cit.

7. Quoted in Kizilos, P., 'Crazy about empowerment', op. cit.

8. Pickard, J., 'The real meaning of empowerment', op. cit.

9. 'Empowerment, a leap of faith?', *Management Training*, August 1993

10. Finegan, J., 'People power', *Inc*, July 1993.

3
HOW DOES ORGANIZATIONAL STRUCTURE SUPPORT EMPOWERMENT GOALS?

No youngster today should dream of becoming a corporate vice president by the time he is 50. By the time he is 50 corporate bureaucracies will no longer exist.

Norman McRae in The Economist

A higher order body should not take unto itself responsibilities which properly belong to a lower order body

Papal Encyclical, 1941

Make every decision as low as possible in the organisation. The charge of the Light Brigade was ordered by an officer who wasn't there looking at the territory.

Robert Townsend, former CEO, Avis

The age of the hierarchy is over.

Corning chairman and chief executive, James R Houghton

Any successful approach to enhancing empowerment within an organization has to tackle a number of strands simultaneously – changing attitudes and behaviours at all levels of the organization, providing people with the training and information they need to take on more responsibility, and removing the organizational barriers to empowerment.

These barriers are for the most part the weighty bureaucracy and slow decision-making characteristic of traditional hierarchical organizations. Removing these barriers is a critical part of empowerment – there are few, if any, examples of truly empowered organizations operating with a traditional hierarchical structure.

Many companies, however, attempt to implement an empowerment strategy with their existing structure largely in place or only partially adapted. These 'full steam ahead empowerment programmes,' notes Christopher Lorenz of *The Financial Times*, 'have developed a nasty habit of hitting the organizational buffers after several years.'[1]

This is not surprising. Leaving organizational buffers in place violates a basic tenet of change: structure must follow strategy. If a company's strategy is to empower its people, then it must develop the structure that will best deliver it. Attempting to empower within the limits imposed by an existing, or slightly altered, structure will allow an organization to achieve at best a part measure of empowerment.

Management writer Tom Peters argues that the only way to make the whole change process work is to transform every aspect of the organization simultaneously:

> Most people who undertake [empowerment initiatives] do not take them all the way. You have to change the concept of the job, the working environment, the structure, hierarchy and communications channels all simultaneously. How long does it take? Either a weekend or for ever, because if you don't do the thing quickly you'll never get it done. You'll always just be part way there.

Ideally, an empowerment initiative would involve dismantling and rebuilding the structure from scratch. Managers would not, as so many have done, simply remove layers. Rather they would define, or redefine, the purpose of the organization and the purpose of each of the roles within it. They would then put together a structure that would best enable both the company and individuals within it to fulfil their respective purposes.

Few companies have changed to this extent, but those that have are now reaping the rewards. A prime example is Semco Brazil, a small São Paulo-based manufacturer of industrial equipment, which has created for itself a virtual cult status by doing away with its hierarchy. President Ricardo Semler (though he prefers the title 'counsellor') sacked his entire senior management team on his first day at work. He went on to cut 12 management layers to three and replace a rigid hierarchical pyramid structure with a flat structure where all report to the centre.

Does it work? Well it doesn't seem to have done any harm. Ninety-three per cent of the workforce responded to a survey that they were well motivated and proud to come to work. The company has grown eleven-fold since the late 1980s, despite Brazil's chaotic, inflation-ridden economic climate.[2]

In reality, of course, organizational structures are not easily taken apart and rebuilt, and most organizations find they have no choice but to alter their strategy and structure simultaneously.

Many are altering their structures anyway, but for reasons other than empowerment. During the 1980s and especially the 1990s, companies have been flattening their pyramids and cutting out layers of middle management in order to cut costs, speed up decision-making and become more flexible and competitive. They then discovered that, without a hierarchy, they could no longer operate in time-honoured hierarchical fashion – they needed empowerment to make the new structure work.

As consultant Dean Berry of management consultants Gemini says:

> Companies may not start out with empowerment as a goal, but when they strip levels out, try to compress time to market and redesign other processes, they end up with it. Even with advanced information technology, you can't really run a delayered organization by command and control. The people route is more timely, simpler, more cost effective, and less risky.[3]

Besides being badly out of fashion, hierarchy doesn't work for modern organizations because most of us need the cooperation of people who we can't command and control anyway, adds Jeffrey Pfeffer of the Stanford Business School.

> We depend on people whom we cannot command, reward or punish even if we wanted to. Even the authority of a chief

executive is not absolute, since there are groups outside the focal organization that control the ability to get things done. And if something is accomplished solely or primarily through hierarchical authority, what happens if the person at the apex of the pyramid is incorrect? What if that person's insight or leadership begins to fail?[4]

THE RIGHT SHAPE FOR EMPOWERMENT

Hierarchy is not completely incompatible with empowerment. As consultant Wally Cork points out, during the 1960s and 1970s a number of companies, notably ICL, had immense success with empowerment initiatives – then called job enrichment – with their hierarchical structures very much in place. 'It is not always necessary to dismantle and rebuild a structure,' he says. 'The best shape for any organization is the one that helps it to achieve the results sought.'

The best shape for empowerment, then, is whatever allows and encourages people to take responsibility. Generally, though, the empowering organization is thought of as being flat, broken into small semi-independent units tied to the centre by a small number of control and support systems. Communications systems are horizontal rather than vertical and command paths run so that empowered teams are answerable to their internal customers rather than to their boss.

The 'right' shape for empowerment depends on the purpose to which is it be put, stresses Coverdale's Richard Carver.

The critical thing to take into account in restructuring, or indeed in any step taken towards creating an empowered organization, is that of purpose. What exactly are we trying to accomplish at individual, team and organizational level? How do these purposes fit together and interact, and therefore what can individuals do to improve their own position, the team's position and the organization's position?

In bureaucratic organizations, there is frequently clarity of role, but little sense of team or company purpose. In empowered companies, people can readily assume someone else's role (so roles tend to be less distinct) and they are guided in doing so by their understanding of the larger picture.

The *Financial Times'* Lorenz describes his vision of an empowering structure:

- ❏ Instead of a series of levels which command and control the one immediately beneath them, power and information on many issues must be delegated, decentralized and diffused.

- ❏ Trust must be established between bosses, peers and subordinates.

- ❏ Individual effort within narrow departmental boundaries must be replaced by cross-functional teams.

- ❏ Instead of information being withheld at each successive level in the hierarchy, it must become shared – or, at least, accessible – through networking.

- ❏ The new structure invariably means fewer managers, each with wider responsibilities. 'Companies are abandoning the old principle that a span of control of between five and 15 people is the most anyone can manage effectively,' writes Lorenz. 'Many managers used to argue that as few as eight was the maximum. Instead, they are installing what Peter Drucker calls "spans of empowerment" of well above 20, in which the manager's role shifts from controller to coach, or mentor.'[5]

The right shape for empowerment must of course take into account the needs of customers. A traditional organizational chart, and even that of many de-layered organizations, usually appears as a pyramid, with executives at the top and customers at the bottom.

Some empowered and customer-responsive organizations have attempted to dispense with this structure, forming instead organizations based on the needs of customers. Many have simply tried to turn the pyramid on its head, putting, at least figuratively, customers at the top of the structure, customer-facing staff beneath them and those further from the customers, such as top executives, towards the bottom. It sounds impressive, but the overall shape of the organization and the systems within it probably don't undergo the radical rethinking that genuine empowerment demands.

One large French multinational adopted the upturned hierarchy approach under the enthusiastic proselytizing of its chief executive. But very little changed in terms of reporting structures or the customer interface, and the CEO's own behaviour remained highly autocratic. The organization did decentralize in a series of centrally inspired convulsions, but this simply added to the confusion. The upturned pyramid ended up in the wastepaper basket when the CEO was prised out of his job.

Paradoxically, however, empowerment did happen in some of the decentralized subsidiaries, where local management made their own decisions about appropriate structures. Although they largely ignored the upturned pyramid, it had created the opportunity for them to experiment quietly and successfully on their own.

More radical empowering structures include the Bull's Eye, the Amoeba, the Star, the Boundaryless organization or even, the Chemical Soup organization.

❑ **The Bull's Eye**: the next stage on from a flat hierarchy, this puts customers in the middle, and builds the organization around their needs. The Bull's Eye does away with the idea of hierarchy, and instead places roles according to their importance to the customers. Customer-facing staff are, after customers, the most central, with those further from the customers radiating further from the centre. Bull's Eye organizations tend to concentrate on empowering their front-line people, but many have had problems extending the same level of empowerment to the back room.

❑ **The Amoeba**: tomorrow's organizations may be more like these, constantly changing their external shape and dividing into new small units. Once the organization reaches a certain size, the new growth is hived off to become a separate business unit.

An Amoeba organization, like any structure, has its weaknesses. Charles Handy cites an example of a furniture company that opted to grow outwards, but not upwards. No business unit would contain more than 100 people. So as the company prospered, it built new factories and mini-businesses, each autonomous, each responsible for generating its own customers and expertise, each remitting its profits to the centre and drawing on the centre, and the others, only if needed. The system worked well in the days of heady growth, but come the recession and the need to allocate scarce resources, there was no one left with the power, authority, or knowledge to make strategic decisions. Left to themselves, the locals could not think globally, and on occasion five separate business units would be found competing against each other for the same order.[6]

❑ **The Star**: this form is occasionally adopted by organizations that serve a small number of very important customers. These companies virtually become part of their clients' organizations, often working on the customers' site, and build their whole organization around the clients' needs. As a result, Star organizations have to give staff a great deal of local autonomy.

Systems consultancy Perot Systems, for example, sends staff to work on its clients' premises and has almost no central organization of its own. To make this work, Perot has had to create a flexible hierarchy within its clients' structures, and has empowered its people to respond, not just to clients' needs, but also to clients' organizational culture.

❑ **The Boundaryless organization**: like the Star, this is most often seen in organizations, such as consultancies, that work very closely with their clients. It goes further than the Star, however, in that it is so responsive to customers that the barriers between customer and supplier become so vague as to be meaningless. Staff in boundaryless organizations must be empowered to respond completely to the needs of customers.

❑ **The Chemical Soup organization**: in this still relatively rare structure, teams evolve for specific projects, then dissolve into new combinations as needed. Management is just another area of expertise to be pulled into the team. Power resides in individual and team capabilities and in networks of trust.

THE RIGHT CULTURE FOR EMPOWERMENT

Structural changes alone will have no effect without a strongly shared organizational culture. Says Richard Carver: 'Unless you have a culture that recognizes the need to change autocracy into participation and cooperates, at an individual level, in making it happen, then structural changes simply do not work.'

On the other hand, if people share a common set of goals, a common perspective on what to do and how to accomplish it, and a common vocabulary that allows them to coordinate their behaviour, then command and hierarchal authority play a much smaller role. People will be able to work cooperatively without waiting for orders from the upper levels of the company.

The most obvious (and, in truly empowered companies, the most superficial) aspect of empowerment is a lack of outward signs of status and hierarchy. An empowered organization will, for example, typically operate on a first name basis between people, even if there are several layers between them, and regardless of the national cultural norms. There are few management privileges, such as reserved parking spaces or a separate canteen. People from different functions mix easily. White collar and blue collar workers are given equal status, and the physical work environment is taken seriously.

At BA's new maintenance plant in Cardiff, for example, opened on a greenfield site in 1993, all staff from the receptionist to the managing director spend at least one day in every quarter on the hangar floor working on aircraft. And all staff, including executives, clock in and wear identical white boiler suits.

At Semco Brazil, there are no secretaries or receptionists. Everyone, even senior executives, does his or her own photocopying and faxing.

At the UK operation of food manufacturer Mars, all directors, as well as shift workers, have to clock on. There are no car parking privileges for directors or managers; they battle with the masses for space. To ensure there is no 'them and us' situation, every member of staff is known as an 'associate'.[7]

Cultural details can also be taken to a ridiculous extent in the opposite extreme. One finance company's supplies department has to know the job classification of an employee before it can deliver a new chair. There are flimsy chairs for typists, more comfortable ones for operators and supervisors, and big cushy ones for managers. 'It's ridiculous. One of the typists borrowed an operator's chair when he was away and it was taken away from her – it's part of corporate policy,' says one employee.

There is, however, clearly more to company culture than such symbolic manifestations as single status canteens and managing directors with first names. After all, whether they are called associates, counsellors or bosses, a manager by any other name must still, on occasion, make some unpopular decisions.

According to Mars corporate affairs manager Locksley Ryan, asking what benefits can be gained by such cultural details misses the point: 'All I can say is, there is a style of operation at Mars, which has grown out of treating everybody the same.'[8]

Mars' culture of equality and individualism has undoubtedly been successful. Jonathan Cable, until recently a middle manager in the sales division of the company, told *The Director*: 'Mars pays its employees a lot of money and it gives them a lot of training in the belief that they can then go off and make decisions,' he says. 'There's very little bureaucracy, it's very hands on. And that motivates. You feel one step closer to running your own business. And above photocopiers there are charts showing return on total assets, there are turnover charts to increase awareness of what rota means, and how we can improve it.'[9]

An empowered culture is an intangible thing. It is not something that can be simply designed or purchased. It can, however, be sensed. And, as shown by companies like Mars and Semco, it can make the difference between empowering, and simply restructuring.

Any organizational culture is made up of a set of under-stood, but not necessarily voiced, assumptions and accepted ideas about 'how things are done around here'. In an empowered culture it is made clear in day-to-day interac-tions that everyone's work and ideas are valued, and that risk-taking and novel ideas are looked for and rewarded. Managers do not assume workers are mostly motivated by money and constructive dissent is welcome.

An empowered culture does have a physical manifestation. To some managers it must look like hell. There are generally few physical, functional or hierarchical barriers. People move around to where they need to be to get things done. At Oticon, a Copenhagen based manufacturer of hearing aids, whose radical structure is described in more detail in Chapter 9, there are no office walls, or even desks. Every employee has a portable workstation that he or she wheels to where they need to work that day. Staff have to be mobile because their job roles are fluid. They work where they are needed on any given day. 'It looks to the outsider like a form of organized chaos,' says managing director Lars Kolind. 'But it's an organized chaos that works.'

The sound of empowerment too, is chaotic, at least to an outsider because, in preference to communicating through formal meetings and memos, people talk to each other. As Nissan Motor GB Ltd's personnel manager Anthony Eastwood describes it: 'If someone's got something to say to a col-league, they're encouraged to say it, not send out a snotty memo copied to all and sundry.'

Formal meetings are rarely called in empowered organiza-tions. Rather, they tend to spring up when people need to talk to one another. At Semco, for example, managing direc-tor Ricardo Semler has a habit of walking into colleagues' offices at random, sitting on the edge of the desk and eaves-dropping.

The feel of an empowered workplace is noticeably different from that of a traditional organization. William Byham describes it as something like an electrical charge. Byham's seismic imagery might be a bit excessive, but the feeling of being excited and involved in one's work is very real in empowered organizations. In such companies there is a conspicuous absence of fear and self-protection, there is an open exchange of ideas and a good dose of constructive conflict. Ideas spark off one another, people do not cover their backs and there is a charge in the atmosphere.

Some companies have tried to measure this charge. Among them is Frizzell Financial Services, one of the first companies to use Saville and Holdsworth's corporate culture questionnaire. The questionnaire measures, among other things, whether people feel empowered or not, as revealed by their scores on the job involvement dimension. The Frizzell survey showed a score of seven out of ten for job involvement for its recently empowered pilot teams, and four out of ten for the rest of the workforce.[10] Though the results are encouraging, the higher scores may have come down to the pilot teams feeling specially selected – the Hawthorne effect, under which any change that suggests care and attention from management may temporarily improve productivity, may have been evidenced here.

However, even the inspiring atmosphere of an empowered culture needs some structure to make it work, argues Pfeffer:

> Without denying the efficacy and importance of vision and culture, it is important to recognize that implementation accomplished through them can have problems. Building a shared conception of the world takes time and effort. There are instances when the organization is in crisis or confronts situations in which there is simply not sufficient time to develop shared premises about how to respond. For this very reason, the military services rely not only on techniques that build loyalty and *esprit de corps*, but also on a hierarchical chain of command and a tradition of obeying orders.[11]

HOW TO CREATE AN EMPOWERING STRUCTURE

Break the business into groups, by customer, or product

Digital Equipment has turned its regional operations in the UK from monolithic departments into 50 small businesses of between 30 and 50 people. Leading each unit is an entrepreneur empowered to run the business as if it were his or her own. Instead of the normal reporting structure, Digital assigns each small business a senior management 'coach'. Coaches are available to give advice and to ensure that units stay small.

In 1993, JCB, the UK's largest construction equipment company, reorganized its 300 employees into separate product divisions and profit centres. Each of the new divisions now has exclusive responsibility for the future of the main product lines. The aim was to create multidisciplinary teams which will sit together and concentrate solely on one product line. The hope is that by identifying more closely with a particular product, employees at all levels will understand the need for increased profitability and be encouraged to participate in achieving it.

Risks inherent in the new structure include dissipation of the company's buying power for parts, or duplicating contact with dealers, but the benefits of the new organization are already coming through: 'We can move faster. The incentive to look at new ideas is much greater,' says Mike Butler, who runs the new Loadall division.

John Appleby, who is in charge of the wheeled loader ranges, says there were initial question marks about whether the new structure could make a difference. 'But we now have much more of a team spirit. The one thing in my team's mind is wheeled loaders.' Already the new approach has led to an improvement in quality and has spurred suggestions from the team about modifications.[12]

Elida Gibbs, a subsidiary of Unilever, experienced impressive improvements in productivity and customer service standards after introducing shopfloor level teamworking in 1988 but, as experience with the new approach grew, managers became aware they needed to go still further.

They realized that the traditional division of the company into separate functions, such as research or distribution, had become a serious handicap. By compartmentalizing management, the organizational structure was frustrating efforts to speed up innovation and increase flexibility. In the autumn of 1992, management was restructured into teams, and managers' roles were redefined on the basis of core business processes, such as the supply chain (manufacturing and logistics) and commercial affairs. These 'seamless teams', as Tony Burgmans, director of Unilever's worldwide personal products business calls them, are intended to involve all parts of the business in decisions at every stage.

According to Helmut Ganser, Elida Gibbs' chairman, the new managerial rank of brand development manager is the linchpin of the system. These managers are the prime movers behind product innovation and have wide authority to pull together the technical and management resources they need to see projects through.

In April 1993, Elida Gibbs launched the first product of the new system: an aerosol deodorant called Brut Aquatonic. It was developed in less than six months, half as long as would have been needed previously. Burgmans reckons the development time today could be as little as three months. But he stresses the biggest advantage of the reorganization is that it enables the company to undertake more ambitious projects, rather than just to keep doing the same things more quickly.[13]

De-layer

Does de-layering make empowerment possible, by freeing up the structure, or does empowerment make de-layering possible by getting staff to take on management responsibilities? Companies are cutting back on middle management ranks to cut costs, while empowering their subordinates to take up the decision-making slack. All of which begs the question: which came first? Are we sacking managers because staff are more empowered, or empowering staff because we need someone to do the work?

Bernard Taylor of Henley Management College feels it is all too often the latter: 'Empowerment has come in at the same time as a vast amount of restructuring has taken place. Two layers of management have been taken out and employees are now being empowered to do three times the amount of work they did before.'

Some organizations find these two motives for de-layering – cost cutting and empowerment – can be in conflict.

However, according to Carver: 'If we get into a conflict between cost reduction and empowerment, then we haven't understood empowerment.'

Consultant Gillian Laidlaw agrees:

> If an organization has to cut costs and get rid of staff, then it is the wrong time to introduce an empowerment initiative. The environment is not supportive enough and people will be terrified of taking risks. A company must get the pain out of the way and then set about making a positive future for the remaining people.

At Harvester Restaurants, as with many companies, empowerment has been inextricably linked to de-layering, and as such was regarded as highly threatening by many staff. When empowerment was introduced in 1992, a layer of management was taken out in the restaurants. Each restaurant now has a branch manager, as well as a coach who handles all training and some other personnel issues. Everyone else is a team member of some description.[14] (See Chapter 9 for details of Harvester's empowerment programme.)

According to Carver:

> Removing layers of management may reduce bureaucracy, but it also reduces the amount of time managers have to coach, train and communicate. They desperately need empowerment in these circumstances. Without it, you have more and more power focused in fewer and fewer people in a flatter and flatter organization in which, without empowerment, the very few people at the very top will have to think of all the ideas for beneficial change. Patently this will not work in today's society.

De-layering can also reduce middle managers' motivation and commitment by taking away what is dearest to many of them – their prospects for promotion. A flat but empowered organization risks having trained, motivated and capable people with no opportunity for advancement. It's a big risk: even if ambitious people don't feel their own jobs are under threat, they may resent the severely reduced promotion prospects, and may question the company's commitment to them and their own commitment to the company.

That commitment is essential, says Ralph Stayer, chief

executive of Johnsonville Foods: 'Flattening pyramids doesn't work if you don't transfer the power too. Before, I didn't have power because I had people wandering around not giving a damn. Real power is getting people committed.'[15]

One somewhat cynical solution companies apply is job title inflation. According to Adrian Furnham, head of the business psychology unit at University College London:

> Flat organizations are under pressure to invent new titles to keep their ambitious staff happy. Many people eager to satisfy their unquenchable self-esteem thirst are happy to accept an improved job title in lieu of a sizeable salary increase. Some companies, in a spirit of crypto-egalitarianism, have chosen to withdraw in-house signs of rank and privilege while at the same time doubling the number of people with manager, director or some such title in the organization.[16]

Others take a more constructive approach. At Fitcorp Inc, a Boston-based fitness centre operator, for example, the management team realized that not all exercise physiologists want to be (or will succeed as) managers.

> So they've added a career track that allows employees to stay on the business's programme side and still get ahead. Senior exercise physiologist John Furey, for example, has been with Fitcorp for five years and professes no desire to go into management. Instead, he has expanded his role to include advising the industry's trade association and conducting health seminars at corporations.[17]

We will look at horizontal career moves in more depth in Chapter 8.

Parcel out support functions to front-line teams

Semco's Ricardo Semler slashed his company's personnel department from 45 people to two, cut corporate staff in legal, accounting and marketing functions by 75 per cent and disposed of the data processing, training and quality control departments altogether.

Semler believes that functions such as personnel, auditing and marketing have traditionally been created in response to line managers, failure to solve their own problems. 'The perfect human resources situation is one where there is no human resources department: it is a sign that the human resources problems are being dealt with by people in the line and not being diverted into a separate areas.'[18]

Make communications flow across rather than up and down

You can only expect people to take authority and make decisions if they have the information they need. Information has to go to the person who owns the problem, not to his or her manager or an off-line department. Where practicable, managers should ensure that all the data referring to a problem is handed over to the employees concerned and that they are given the freedom to follow any avenue they need to for further information.

At Ericsson GE's Lynchburg Virginia plant, the hierarchy has been successfully bypassed in an experiment, though at the time of writing it had yet to be implemented across the company. Normally, the purchasing system involves a convoluted hierarchical chain in which the employee tells her supervisor, who tells her manager, who then tells Dick Hunter, Ericsson's director of procurement and logistics, about any faulty parts. Hunter then calls the supplier's salesperson, who calls his manager, who calls her supervisor, who finally tells the line employee at the other end that the parts are defective. But some line employees from Ericsson GE are now directly calling the line worker at the supplier when faulty parts are discovered. Hunter hopes to see this done more often in the future.

The kind of interlinking communication flow seen at Ericsson GE is typical in the few organizations that have taken empowering structures one step further. These are the kind of organizations that Peter Drucker describes in his book *The New Realities*.[19]

Drucker predicts that, in knowledge-based companies, hierarchies will give way to something resembling a symphony orchestra, with dozens or even hundreds of specialists reporting directly to the conductor/chief executive. Others with a less poetic bent describe the change as business process re-engineering.

The *Financial Times*' Lorenz explains:

> Traditionally in organizations each function has its own hierarchy down and up which communications has to pass before it is transferred to the next department. Most western organizations have been only partly successful in bridging such vertical structures either with permanent matrices or temporary project teams, task forces or overlays.
>
> Re-engineering, or core process redesign, goes a big step further. It transforms such processes into ones which flow permanently across the relevant departments at the appropriate level, usually pretty low. This involves not only de-layering those departments, and removing front-line staff from them, but sometimes breaking them up. Only a handful of companies, such as Taco Bell, and the Astra Merck pharmaceutical alliance in the US, and National and Provincial Building Society (N&P) in Britain, have yet gone to the extent of revolutionizing structures at the top, as well as lower down, and giving process responsibilities not just to junior and middle managers, but also to senior executives.

According to Frank Ostroff, a consultant with McKinsey and Co. in New York, a horizontal structure embraces not only core process redesign, it also provides the overall structure, reward systems and multi-purpose skill training needed to link all its teams together so that they perform miracles for the customer without creating process barriers which are just as harmful as the old departmental ones. Ostroff maintains that even a decade from now, only about 10 per cent of companies will be fully horizontal and that most will retain some degree of verticality. 'This is realistic', writes Lorenz, 'and shows off horizontal for what it will remain for most organizations – optimistic or misleading.'[20]

Business academics Frank Shipper and Charles C Manz describe an alternative structure – the lattice structure. In most companies,

> employee self-management is introduced in organizations through the establishment of formally designated empowered work teams. When employees are hired, they are assigned to a work team as a condition of their employment. But the lattice approach promises to deliver many of the advantages and

benefits of formally established empowered employee work teams – but without formally designated teams. Instead, the whole work operation becomes essentially one large empowered team in which everyone is individually self managing and can interact directly with everyone else in the system.[21]

This is what happens at WL Gore and Associates, a company that relies on self-developing teams without managers or bosses, but with lots of leaders.

First, work unit size was an issue. Once, according to Shipper and Manz, when Bill Gore was taking his usual walk through the plant, he suddenly realized he did not know everyone. The team had become too big. As a result, the company developed a policy that no facility could have more than 150 to 200 employees, thus giving birth to a distinctive expansion strategy: 'Get big by staying small.'

But the lattice structure goes far beyond manageable team size. The primary characteristics of this structure are:

❑ lines of communications are direct – person-to-person – with no intermediary

❑ there is no fixed or assigned authority

❑ there are sponsors, not bosses

❑ natural leadership is defined by followership

❑ objectives are set by those who must make them happen

❑ tasks and functions are organized through commitments.

The structure within the lattice is complex and evolves from interpersonal interactions, self-commitment to responsibilities known within the group, natural leadership, and group-imposed discipline.

Another phenomenon within the lattice is the constant formation of temporary cross-area groups. The cross-level and cross-functional contact created by this structure enables all kinds of teams to spring up as specific needs arise. Associates can team up with other associates, regardless of area, to get the job done. When a puzzled interviewer told Bill Gore that he was having trouble understanding how planning and accountability worked, Gore replied with a grin: 'So am I. You ask me how it works... the answer is, it works, every which way.' It is, he says, based on the natural, underground, lattice that occurs in every organization. 'It's where the news spreads like lightning, where people can go around the organization to get things done.'

'The lattice structure should, however, be considered with some caution,' warn Shipper and Manz. 'Just as with any other new management approach, it should be evaluated in terms of its fit with an organization's culture and objectives.' Bill Gore defends the approach, but with sensitivity to its alleged limitations:

> I'm told from time to time that a lattice organization can't meet a crisis well because it takes too long to reach a consensus when there are no bosses. But this isn't true. Actually, a lattice, by its very nature, works particularly well in a crisis. A lot of useless effort is avoided because there is no rigid management hierarchy to conquer before you can attack a problem.

Other critics include outsiders who had problems with the idea of no titles. Sarah Clifton, an associate at the Flagstaff facility, was being pressed by some outsiders as to what her title was. She made one up and had it printed on some business cards – Supreme Commander. When Bill Gore learned what she did, he loved it and recounted the story to others.

A customer points to a more important limitation: 'After you've established a relationship with someone about product quality, you can call up one day and suddenly find that someone new to you is handling your problem. It's frustrating to find a lack of continuity.'

Bill Gore says established companies would find it very difficult to use the lattice. Too many hierarchies would be destroyed. When you move titles and positions and allow people to follow whom they want, it may very well be someone other than the person who has been in charge. 'The lattice works for us, but it's always evolving. You have to expect problems.' He maintained that the lattice system works best when put in place by a dynamic entrepreneur in a start-up company.

Federalism

For large corporations, particularly multinationals, the right shape for empowerment is what Charles Handy calls federalism.[22]

Though usually thought of as a political issue, as a way for large and multicultural countries like Canada or Australia to reap the benefits of both local autonomy and economies of scale, federalism is increasingly being adopted by large, multinational corporations. 'Federalism answers the need for companies to be both big, for economies of scale, and small, for independence, flexibility and innovative thinking,' says Handy.

> In a federal system, power is a fluid thing, placed, or left, where it is most needed and moved according to the task or purpose at hand. This is what makes it different from both a traditional conglomerate structure, where the centre merely acts as a banker to the separate businesses, and decentralization, where individual businesses act so independently they lose the advantages of scale.
>
> For individuals, federalism is a way to have one's cake and eat it too: they can have the freedom and flexibility of autonomous work groups, but also be part of a larger family that can provide the resources, career opportunities, and leverage that comes with size. It's a way to make it big while keeping it small – and independent.

To make it work, says Handy, it is necessary to follow a number of key principles:

❑ Power belongs to the lowest possible point in the organization, and the centre governs only with the consent of the governed.

❑ This principle, called subsidiarity, has to be formalized. It has to be clear who can do what, how power is to be balanced, and whose authority counts where.

❑ Subsidiarity requires intelligence and information, real-time data that is broad enough to give a total picture but detailed enough to pinpoint decision points.

❑ Interdependence: the states of a federation stick together because they need one another as much as they need the centre. Interdependence is achieved partly through the reserve powers of the centre, partly by locating services or facilities needed by all in the territory of one or two. Federalism encourages combination when and where appropriate, but not centralization.

❑ A proper federation needs a common law, language, and currency – a uniform way of doing business.

❑ Twin citizenship: individuals within the company can feel loyal to their work group and to the organization as a whole without conflict, just as an ardent Texan sees no conflict with being an American.

❑ Separation of powers keeps management monitoring and governance in segregated units. According to Handy, the management, monitoring and governance of a business are increasingly seen as separate functions to be done by separate bodies, even if some of the membership of those bodies overlaps.

THE ROLE OF UNIONS IN RESTRUCTURING

According to a report by the Involvement and Participation Association,[23] a British organization devoted to encouraging employee involvement in industry, 'trade unions are having to come to terms with the fact that they are no longer the sole channel of representation. The individual employee is seen by many employers as the new industrial relations entity around whom the fundamental manager–employee relationship will be built'.

Empowerment does not, however, spell the end of unions. Barry and Irving Bluestone argue that unions can help support empowerment initiatives.[24] According to their research,

participation turns out to work best when it is organized jointly between union and management and when workers have a voice independent from management that cannot be unilaterally stifled. Mixing adversarial and cooperative relations – negotiated within a context where employees are represented by legally recognized unions – proves to be the most successful form of employee involvement for all participants.

Over the past two decades, unions within key industries have widened the traditional workplace contract – which represents the standard adversarial positions between labour and management over wages, benefits, and working conditions – to include employee involvement in workplace decisions.

The two Bluestones see the unfolding of a three-track system of labour management relations, which runs neatly parallel to Bowen and Lawler's three levels of empowerment described in Chapter 1.

❏ Track I is the traditional labour contract with a carefully spelled out grievance procedure.

❏ Track II provides for employee involvement in the decision-making process, empowering individual employees to help determine workplace issues.

❏ Track III is characterized by the establishment of joint union–management committees empowered to deal with specific issues of mutual concern – problems of quality, efficiency, health and safety and a host of other issues that previously fell within the sole domain of management.

The Bluestones report on an extreme example of effective union involvement: Saturn Corp, a joint venture between the United Auto Workers (UAW) and General Motors to conceive, design, and build automobiles with full union participation. The union is intimately involved in an extensive array of strategic decisions. Management and workers in joint committees designed the physical plant, chose the technology to be used, devised marketing strategies and recruited the workforce. A committee of 99 – 55 from the union and 44 from management – established the guidelines governing the decision-making process. The negotiated labour contract with the UAW is unique in that its entire structure is predicated on joint decision-making, involving everyone from the president of the corporation to the employee on the shop floor. It stipulates that any party may block a potential decision but that this party must search for an alternative. And it specifies that problems are to be solved through a form of continuing negotiation, which includes the right to strike.

What is special about Saturn, however, is that participation does not stop at the shop floor. For example, the actual design of the Saturn automobile was determined jointly, as was the pricing strategy. The Saturn automobile was named the best buy of any passenger vehicle selling for under $10,000 by *Car and Driver* magazine in 1992. The major dealer complaint is that they cannot get enough to satisfy demand.

The technology is not unusual, and radical marketing successes are not really the norm at GM, but, write Bluestone and Bluestone:

> When one visits the plant itself, one begins to understand the secret. Virtually every worker at Saturn feels that he or she is responsible for the success of the division. Workers constantly make suggestions for improving styling, engineering, and manufacturing techniques; and each pays diligent attention to the quality of every part that passes his or her work station.

Saturn, however, stops short of the complete joint participation that the Bluestones feel is the key to success on a grander scale. For example, the union's role at Saturn is still restricted to consultation on design and engineering. The Saturn division must get approval from GM to introduce a new car model, and if it feels short-changed in the amount of capital investment allocated by GM's board of directors, the division is forbidden to seek funding from outside sources.

Expanding beyond the Saturn model requires a new level of both labour empowerment and worker responsibility within the firm. Towards those ends, Bluestone and Bluestone propose the development of an 'enterprise compact' that would specify joint labour–management action over all decision of the firm, both workplace and strategic. Such a compact might include provisions on union management joint productivity goals, product quality to be a strikable issue, profit sharing and an agreement that all strategic decisions should be made through joint action.

CONCLUSION

A critical trap to avoid in any empowerment initiative is confusing restructuring and empowerment. Restructuring alone will not empower an organization. It will only help make empowerment possible by removing some of the barriers to it.

Nor is empowerment a step-by-step process starting with restructuring. No one has ever created an empowered organization by flattening the structure on Monday, changing job descriptions on Tuesday, and letting them at it on Wednesday. Many companies find it can take up to ten years to change a company's culture, organizational design and management practices enough to create a truly empowered organization.

Even if empowerment was a step-by-step process, a flattened, de-layered organization would still have a long way to go. To create an empowered organisation it is also necessary to change attitudes and behaviours, and to provide people with the skills they need to function in the new structure.

Structures (and empowerment itself) can only be effective if people working in them have the skills to make use of them. In a fluid, flat, empowered structure, individuals will be called upon to use skills such as influencing, negotiating, problem-solving and teamworking, possibly for the first time and at much lower levels of the organization.

In the following chapter we will look at how they can start to develop some of these skills, as we approach developing the core unit for empowerment – operational level teams.

References

1. Lorenz, C., 'Power to the people', *Financial Times,* 30 March 1992.

2. Hall, L., 'The boss from Brazil', *Personnel Today,* 26 October 1993.

3. Lorenz, C. 'Nuts and bolts of giving power to the people', *Financial Times,* 21 Sept, 1992.

4. Pfeffer, J., 'Power: the not-so-dirty secret to success in

organizations', *Stanford Business School Magazine*, March 1992.

5. Lorenz, C., 'Uphill struggle to become horizontal', *Financial Times,* 5 November 1993.

6. Handy, C., 'Balancing corporate power: a new federalist paper', *Harvard Business Review,* November-December 1992.

7. Jackson, S., 'Empowerment to the people?', *Director*, April 1991.

8. Ibid.

9. Ibid.

10. Pickard, J., *'The real meaning of empowerment'*, *Personnel Management*, November 1993.

11. Pfeffer, J., 'Power: The not-so-dirty secret to success', op. cit.

12. Baxter, A., 'Selectors' choice', *Financial Times,* 11 August 1993.

13. De Jonquieres, G., 'A clean break with tradition', *Financial Times*, 12 July 1993.

14. Pickard, J., 'The real meaning of empowerment', op. cit.

15. Stewart, T. A. 'A users guide to power', *Fortune,* 6 November 1989.

16. Furnham, A., 'Job title inflation hits the roof', *Financial Times,* 12 January 1993.

17. Fenn, D. 'Bottoms up', *Inc*, July 1993.

18. Hall, L., 'The boss from Brazil', *Personnel Today,* 26 October 1993.

19. Drucker, P. (1989), *The New Realities,* Heinemann, London.

20. Lorenz, C., 'Uphill struggle to become horizontal', op. cit.

21. Shipper, F. and Manz, C., 'An alternative road to empowerment', *Organizational Dynamics,* June 1990.

22. Handy, C., 'Balancing corporate power', op. cit.

23. *Towards Industrial Partnerships, A New Approach to Relationships at Work,* The Involvement and Participation Association, London, 1992.

24. Bluestone, B. and Bluestone, I., 'Workers (and managers) of the world unite', *Technology Review*, November/December 1992.

4
BUILDING AND OPER-ATING EMPOWERED TEAMS

I think of the company as a volleyball team. It takes three hits to get the ball over the net, and it doesn't matter who hits it'
Lori Sweningson, CEO of Job Boss Software Inc.

Gut feeling tells me 90 per cent of teams working together could improve their productivity if they could improve their team building skills.
Consultant Bernard Wynne.

This is a lovely team, I wouldn't want to let it down.
Teamworker at Britvic

Self-directed teams are one element – and in many companies the most important step – towards an empowered work culture. Self-directed teams are small groups of employees with day-to-day responsibility for managing themselves and their work. Team members handle job assignments, plan and schedule work, make production-related decisions and resolve problems. Many tasks, such as recruitment and scheduling, that were previously allocated to managers and supervisors can be given over to these teams. As a result, team-centred companies operate with fewer levels of management than conventional organizations and require team members to learn multiple jobs and tasks. And, unlike quality circles and cross-functional task groups, self-directed teams are formal, permanent structures.

Teams play a critical role in empowerment, says Coverdale consultant Keith Edwards, in that they help ensure people cooperate for mutual benefit:

Empowerment could be a nuisance without context – without common goals, empowered people could cause havoc. Luckily, there is a natural tendency in human beings to cooperate with each other, so if you increase people's awareness of the importance of teamworking and give them the skills to work together more easily, then they will cooperate happily.

Not all organizations have found teams come together that easily. Many, however, have discovered that there are gains to be made by making teams the productive unit of their operation. For example, after a major restructuring at Dairycrest's Hemel Hempstead Prepack Centre, weekly output of packed cheese went up by 20 per cent, costs of packing decreased by 10 per cent and staff turnover, once very high, was reduced to virtually zero. All this was achieved despite a 40 per cent reduction in managerial staff.

Operations manager Steve Whitmarsh credits the improvement to the teamwork approach, involving both training and changes in working style, introduced at Dairycrest as part of the restructuring:

One of the greatest things has been the personal development of individuals as a result of the team building experience. If I had not seen it happening before my own eyes, I would not have believed it possible. People have taken on the ownership of projects, assumed increased accountability and they have delivered.

Rank Xerox UK has converted its entire customer service division of 2200 people into 205 self-managed work groups. John Prevost, a field supervisor who is coach to a team of 11 engineers servicing photocopying machines, told management writer David Oates that the collective approach leads to greater efficiency:

Some engineers are very fast; others are slow but very thorough. In the past, the slow engineer might have been penalized for not keeping up with productivity targets, but in a team you've got room for both types of people, provided everyone recognizes their individual role. You need a blend, but it is important to point out the strengths and weaknesses so that everyone feels comfortable with what's happening.[2]

To achieve this high degree of awareness, Prevost has introduced a system that allows members of the group to appraise each other's work. The appraisals are done on paper and presented to the employee in question by one assigned team member. Prevost has found that the members of his work group take a more responsible attitude towards performing their jobs than they used to. Problems with servicing customers' machines are now discussed openly, instead of being swept under the carpet.

Shaun Pantling, Rank Xerox's director of customer service, estimates that self-managed work groups will increase the productivity of his division by 25 per cent over three years. Managing director Vernon Zemler says: 'We have basically told the teams to run the business.'

After undergoing a massive training programme established in the early 1980s, teams of employees at the Campbell's Soup plant in Maxton, North Carolina began making traditional management decisions without direct supervision. 'We turned the business over to them,' says the plant manufacturing vice-president. The teams met with vendors, set their own schedules and even proposed capital expenditures, complete with calculations of the rate of return. A new machine suggested by one work team is so productive that it yielded an overall 30 per cent return on its investment. Soon after implementing joint decision-making, the plant achieved a record 16 per cent increase in productivity in a single year.[3]

In 1988, Northern Telecom's 420-employee switching equipment repair facility in Morrisville, North Carolina also began moving toward joint decision-making. Employees are organized into cells that set their own goals for meeting objectives ranging from efficiency targets to turnaround times. Cell members also conduct performance reviews, interview job applicants and set flexible work schedules. Three years after the programme was installed, revenues at the facility were up by 83 per cent, earnings per employee increased by 93 per cent, quality (as measured by returned parts) improved by 51 per cent and customer service satisfaction (as indicated by a reduction in complaints) rose by 65 per cent.[4]

Digital Equipment's plant at Ayr, Scotland has been using high performance work teams since the early 1980s. These teams are so successful they have reduced lead times from about eight weeks to one day. The teams of up to 30 people are multiskilled and can assemble a computer in a day. They are responsible for recruitment, training and discipline as well as order processing. They liaise directly with other departments rather than going through managers, and each member is paid according to the skills he or she has. The manager gives guidance to 250 people and is the last resort for discipline issues that the team cannot cope with.

HOW SELF-DIRECTED TEAMS ARE BEST ORGANIZED, TRAINED AND SUPPORTED

In developing self-directed teams, an organization and its employees must consider:

❑ Where do we start?

❑ How do we select team members?

❑ What training do we need?

❑ How will the formation of teams affect front-line, supervisory and management jobs?

❑ What role will support departments play?

❑ What responsibilities will team leaders take?

❑ Do we need team leaders at all?

Where do we start?

The authors of *New Roles for Managers*, a report by the Work in America Institute of Scarsdale, New York, advise:

❑ Think of teams as independent, entrepreneurial, 'factories within a factory' inside the organization.

❑ Be sure that the team gets the resources it needs to finish the job. If you want to see a frustrated team, don't give it the resources you promised.

❑ Let the team set its own parameters, the 'how to', 'what to', and 'when to'. You set the end point that forces process innovation, but the team determines the inter-mediate milestones.

❑ Then keep out of the way. Let the team make its own decisions. Don't punish risk-takers. Expect problems, even disasters.

Management consultant Bernard Wynne advises a four-step process to help the formation of teams:

1. Ensure each team member has an equal understanding of the purpose of the team and what customers expect of it.

2. Set clear objectives about how to achieve that purpose and meet those expectations.

3. Determine what is preventing the team from achieving that purpose. Barriers typically include: lack of skill, problems in interpersonal relationships among team members, reluctance to share skills and information, and lack of job flexibility.

4. Work to overcome those barriers.

This is not a rapid process, warns Richard Wellins, senior vice-president of the Pennsylvania-based consultancy Development Dimensions International:

> Successful self-directed organizations commonly spend up to 20 per cent of a team member's or leader's time in training activities during the first year of operation. And it can take from 12 months before team start up to two years after to do it properly. Most organizations talk about a time span of two to five years to develop fully empowered teams.[5]

In 1993, OCS Smarts Group, a UK laundry and workwear ser-vice, set out to build a teamworking culture from scratch. It broke up its conventional management and workforce struc-ture into a series of 50 teams or commercial networks as they called them. Each had greater responsibility for and ownership of, its customer base.

Management's role would be to support, coach and act as mentors for the rest of the workforce, who were to become commercial network members.

By mid-1993, 28 commercial networks were in place and at various stages of development. Typically, in one laundry, the concept of commercial networks would be briefed to all staff, starting with local management. The laundry would then be encouraged to work out for itself how best to turn the concept into practice at its own pace. Potential network leaders and members would be involved to learn more about the process of forming their own networks.

Staff have also attended in-house commercial development seminars, to learn the basics of the company's products, services and customer needs. Training in the early days of each network was kept low-key, to avoid being overly prescriptive with tools and techniques and to encourage teams to identify their own training needs. As a result, many have identified visits to customers as a prime requirement in their early days.

One of the first activities of a network is to calculate the value of the business for which it will be responsible. To many, this comes as something of a surprise. Another early task is to come up with quick-fix solutions to problems identified by the team. This builds confidence and encourages the teams to address more demanding customer and business-oriented issues.

The rate at which networks have sought information and progressed their activities has caught management by surprise – so much so that management's speed of response has, in some instances, been the constraining factor. One solution to this has been to invite network leaders to sit in on the existing management meetings so that their needs and progress can be given rapid consideration.[6]

How do we select team members?

When the JCB management team decided to reorganize its 300 employees into separate product divisions and profit centres, its methods were reminiscent of picking sides for basketball. In January 1993 an office wall held the names of all 300 JCB employees. Their individual strengths and weaknesses were discussed and analysed by the management team, as a prelude to reorganizing the main divisions of the

UK's largest construction equipment company. The managing directors of each of the three new divisions were asked to pick their teams. The names on the wall system, 'brought into focus the team players and those who were coasting. Valuable insights were gained on the employees, enabling the three new divisional leaders to take a chance on some people by increasing their responsibilities.'[7]

JCB's management kept in mind what can be too easily forgotten in a rush to teamworking. Teams are made up of individuals, and not all members are going to be equally flexible or keen to take responsibility. One or two uncooperative members can be enough to scupper the productivity of a whole team. This is why some companies have found it necessary to let teams select their own members. At Johnsonville Foods in Wisconsin, for example, some employees were unhappy about fellow workers whose performance was slipshod or indifferent. Convinced that inadequate selection and training of new workers were causing the performance problems, line workers asked to do the selecting and training themselves.

Senior management, realizing that people on the shop floor knew more about shop floor performance than they did, offered to set performance standards, coach staff in confronting poor performers and train them in selection and training procedures. Now, line workers have assumed most of the traditional personnel functions.

Other organizations leave recruitment to managers, but make 'empowerability' part of the selection criteria. It is, according to Coverdale's Richard Carver, possible to recruit for empowerability:

> At its essence, 'empowerability' is the willingness of individuals, under the right circumstances, to take on personal responsibility for improving the situation in which they find themselves. Most companies look for this in recruiting managers and leaders of the future, but it is probably less common to look for this at all levels in a company.
>
> I know some theorists say that, if the culture is right all individuals will accept personal responsibility and become empowered. My experience is that this is not so. Empowerment is a two-way street and some people are more

inclined to accept the personal responsibility that goes with empowerment than others. Such people will prosper most in a culture in which they are encouraged to take risks to improve the way they do their job, praised for the successes they achieve and helped with training so they can work effectively both on their own and with others.

One way to select for empowerability, suggest management academics Frank Shipper and Charles Manz, is to conduct realistic job previews that inform employees about what they're getting into, along with orientation and training to prepare them to deal with high levels of autonomy. 'These are probably essential ingredients for organizations considering adopting a system of empowerment and self-directed teams.'[8]

Another way is to use tests to identify personality characteristics in potential recruits. However, Angela Baron, a policy advisor and occupational psychologist at the Institute of Personnel Management, feels that personality is too complex a measure to find with a single test: 'There are some very good tests, and some very bad ones. To generalize and say all jobs need this score, or these attributes, would be a big mistake.'

To use tests effectively, she says: 'You must start with a job or person specification, define what traits you are looking for, and use tests to determine if that person has those traits. You can't just pick two to three attributes and add them up. What is required depends on the needs of each organization.'

When Neil Roden, a personnel manager, recruited staff for a new customer service centre for the finance company Lloyds Bowmaker, he was looking for 'people who could develop a relationship with customers over the telephone, who could be pleasant, but also firm when they needed to say no.'

Lloyds Bowmaker used a six-stage procedure of interviews, psychometric tests and group dynamics exercises, most of which were designed to seek out these innate abilities and attitudes. Roden believes that this was easier than trying to train an average cross-section of applicants in teamworking and in taking responsibility for customer service. 'We can give people the technical skills,' he says. 'But moulding someone's attitudes is extremely difficult.'

What training do we need?

Employees who become members of self-managed work teams are expected to take on supervisory functions such as the hiring and firing of other team members, negotiating vacation schedules, making decisions about production goals, and so on.

This, as William Byham points out, is not something that can be simply handed over to team members: 'You're dealing with adults who have never done those kinds of things. It's not something where you can just read a book or go to a two-day training seminar or a one-hour motivational programme to learn. There is some real skill development involved to make it work.'

Richard Wellins argues that ineffective training – not supervisory resistance – is the number one barrier to successful team implementation. 'In creating a team oriented environment, the team members themselves should be involved in developing and delivering the training,' he says. 'And don't underestimate the need for new types of training.'

Many organizations underestimate the need for any kind of training. Coverdale consultant Rob Gordon describes an experience he had in helping to build self-directed teams in a manufacturing organization:

> The production director told us he intended to switch to team-working in manufacturing cells. The existing supervisory layer would be replaced by foremen who would become team leaders. 'They might need a little bit of help in adjusting to the changes', he told me.
>
> This was a serious understatement. We met a group of people – the team leaders to be – who could best be described as terrified. All of the familiar props of structure, systems and authority had been knocked away, leaving a void. It required an intensive period of preparation, helping that group build new skills and confidence and then a year working with them and their teams before the organization began to see the hoped-for benefits.

Self-directed teams encourage multiskilling and job rotation, which means a heavy investment in technical training; they call on employees to anticipate and solve workplace problems;

and they also require workers, who in the past had been rewarded for individual performance, to learn to work together as a team. Therefore three categories of skills are essential for effective team performance, says Wellins:

❑ **Job skills**: the technical skills required for job performance.

❑ **Team and interaction skills** such as giving and receiving feedback, handling conflict, valuing diversity, working in teams, and training and coaching other team members.

❑ **Quality and action skills** such as statistical process control (SPC), training in various types of quality tools, techniques for continuous improvement, and troubleshooting, to enable team members to identify and solve problems without recourse to management.

Training works best when provided over time, rather than in one shot, he adds. 'Some organizations offer all their training in four to six week training colleges, which prove difficult for all – especially for production workers used to walking the floor rather than sitting in a classroom.'

Jon Riches, personnel director at Elida Gibbs, the UK personal products subsidiary of Unilever, credits training with the successful introduction of team working at the company's Seacroft plant in 1988:[9] 'The changes would have been absolutely impossible to implement without training – it opened people's minds,' he says. Riches has overseen an increase in the company's training budget from 0.5 per cent to 1.3 per cent of sales since the late 1980s. In 1993, he aimed to give every employee ten days' training.

The training was part of a programme that shifted responsibility for each production line to those working on it. Workers are encouraged to cooperate to solve problems and improve efficiency and are given fuller information about the company's performance and overall strategy.

Initially, the switch faced scepticism from trades union officials and older middle managers. To win acceptance, the company put its 1,000 employees through three-day courses on total quality run by teachers selected from the workforce.

The new approach has produced some big gains. In the past three years, changeover time on one production line has been reduced to less than four hours from a day and a half, while annual lost time accidents at Seacroft have been cut by three quarters. Between 1989 and 1991 pre-tax profits rose by 73 per cent and margins widened from 6.5 to 10 per cent.

'Elida Gibbs' delivery standards used to be dire and their ordering systems archaic,' Michael Rosen, director of non-foods at J. Sainsbury told the *Financial Times*. 'The whole thing was shambolic. They were nearing the point of losing a lot of business.' Now, he says, the company is one of Sainsbury's most efficient suppliers .

Many teams require more that just practical skills training. They also need more general training, or at least practice in, working as a team. Though many consultants and managers argue that this is best done in the work situation, a growing number of companies are using off-site and outdoors training to help bind teams.

At the Swindon-based film manufacturers, Courtaulds Films Polypropylene, after employees had been working in teams for about ten months, the company's 36 operators were sent on a one-day team-building outdoor game. This was preceded by a half-day prebrief and followed by a debriefing.

The ostensible object of the game was for each team to produce a mapped layout of a 90-acre wood, including 35 numbered junctions and to locate some hidden information, all within ten hours. It soon became obvious that the only way to complete the task was to cooperate with one's teammates.

'Unencumbered by the factory environment, the team leaders were able to watch how their people behaved in a team-working situation,' says Coverdale consultant Peter Bennett, who worked with Courtlands on the exercise. Asked what had been the value of the exercise, 95 per cent of the participants said the day had been extremely valuable. The lessons they had learnt gave them insights into how they could be a better team in the workplace. And, because each team leader had previously been through a team leader workshop and spent the ten hours with their teams, he or she had an improved rapport with the group and carried away new ideas on how to further develop the cooperative spirit.

Training should not, however, stop there. 'A critical element in building effective teams and structures is to ensure that learning continues once the teams are in operation,' stresses Coverdale's Gordon. 'Continuous learning forms the basis for continuous improvement, which is itself a cornerstone of empowerment.'

How will the formation of teams affect first-level jobs?

Probably the biggest change required of operators in self-directed teams, besides teamworking itself, is the need to be multiskilled.

Multiskilling, or training in several job areas, is in itself a rewarding business, says Peter Bennett, a Coverdale consultant and an expert in operator development. 'It is a vital part of the process in helping operators realize that they are capable of managing themselves and can be directly accountable for what they do.'

It is not, however, necessary to train all team members in every job to create an effectively multiskilled workforce. Most companies find they must balance the cost of training with the benefits of multiskilling. As one food processing factory manager pointed out: 'The people on the shop floor here think that multiskilling means everybody has to be able to do everything, but we don't need 100 forklift truck drivers. We only need two, and we haven't got the time to train everybody in a skill they are unlikely to use.'

There are various approaches to striking this balance, but most fall into one of three categories:

1. **Job depth**: team members learn a specific process in greater depth. For example, they would first learn to operate a piece of equipment, then move on to perform basic preventive maintenance, and finally advanced maintenance, on that same piece of equipment.

2. **Job breadth:** team members learn all the jobs or tasks required of an entire team. For example, in a car manufacturer, the seat assembly team might have six or seven different production tasks, each performed by one team member. But all team members learn all the tasks. The idea is to encourage staff to be able to do each other's jobs as much as possible.

3. **Vertical skills:** with this third and least common method, team members learn the leadership skills used in all jobs. Examples include troubleshooting techniques, training, safety and leading meetings.

Multiskilling and teamwork is largely credited with the commercial survival of Shell Chemicals' UK site at Carrington, near Manchester. Until 1985, demarcation and restrictive practices were widespread throughout the organization, but were particularly prevalent among the unionized labour in the production and engineering departments. Since the late 1970s, the business performance of the Carrington site had been very poor and, by 1985, the site's future was under serious threat. The workforce had been slashed from 3,000 to 1,200, then cut again to 500.

To ensure survival, these 500 were pledged to work on a highly flexible basis. Who-does-what boundaries vanished between the different types of craft-based and technical work. Working with the City and Guilds of London Institute, Carrington designed a training and accreditation system leading to a multiskill qualification unique in British industry. The new qualification meant that a trained mechanic could, for instance, tackle some electrical work as well. There was also the emergence of the manufacturing technician, a multi-skill role combining the previously separate jobs of operator and craftsman.

The workforce also started to operate in teams, with each team member sufficiently skilled to be able to stand in for his or her team mates when necessary. For example, production staff no longer had to stand by idly while maintenance staff carried out repairs – they now had the skills to pitch in.

Psychological divides between the various skill groups largely disappeared as well. Old complaints like: 'The operators can't operate it', or 'If the engineers had done it properly, it would be OK', are no longer heard.

Other companies have found that psychological divisions are very difficult to overcome. As one supervisor at a major food manufacturer asked: 'Have we got rid of shopfloor demarcations, or just shifted them around? Do people now have mental demarcations instead?'

Multiskilling isn't the only change that teamworking makes to front-line jobs. There are other, less tangible but equally important, changes.

Increased responsibility:

Coverdale consultant Wally Cork tells of his experience working with beverage manufacturer Britvic:

> In the early days, when there was a pile-up on the line, operators further up the line would simply pick up their newspapers and sandwiches and wait patiently for the line to start again. Two years after Britvic had implemented teamworking I was there again and sure enough, the line went berserk. But this time three operators jumped and ran to help the person in the middle sort it all out. To me, that was a fundamental shift. The lesson is: we can help one another. As one operator said: 'This is a lovely team, I wouldn't want to let it down.'

Increased trust and mutual respect

Without the constant threat of management discipline to ensure everyone contributes, team members must trust one another to pull their weight. For example, at Frizzell Financial Services, when the old bonus scheme linked to individual achievement of targets was replaced with bonuses for the best teams, some fast workers felt they were carrying the slow coaches, and didn't like it.[10]

Such grievances can arise, especially where money is involved, but, as Coverdale's Milo Lynch discovered, teamworking and multiskilling can in themselves help break down the barriers of distrust between different job roles:

> At British Cellophane we put people into mixed discipline groups. Operators were working alongside technicians and designers on real technical or production problems. The results were remarkable. Everybody could see how they made a contribution to other functions and relationships throughout the plant became much easier.

Increased willingness to learn from peers and colleagues

Empowered teamworkers soon find both an increased need, and a growing willingness, to rely on their teammates for help and advice. As Julie Cullen, a machine operator at Walkers Smiths' Swansea factory, says: 'The atmosphere here has changed a lot. Now, if I have a problem, I will talk to the other people on my line. I wouldn't really have done that before.'

How will the formation of teams affect supervisory and management jobs?

Supervisors and managers might well ask themselves, says Richard Wellins:

❑   How will I be involved in the self-directed team?

❑   Do I have the right skills to make the transition?

❑   Will I be blamed if things don't work out?

❑   Will I lose my job?

Though managers' roles will be discussed in more detail in Chapter 5, it should be noted here that supervisors and managers will face more change from the introduction of self-directed teams than the team members themselves. As many of their tasks will be taken on by the team, some supervisors and managers will face unemployment, or at least redeployment.

Wellins' research found that 68 per cent of organizations using self-directed teams were able to operate with fewer managers, and 95 per cent of the respondents found this change to be beneficial. At Michelin Tyres for example, there were 38 management positions at one factory in 1990. After the introduction of self-directed teams, there were 18. Others will take on a new role of coach and resource obtainer, providing teams with the support, training and resources they need to do the job.

At Frizzell Financial Services, telesales and service people have always worked in informal teams, and the company did not do away with supervisors when it introduced teamworking into these departments, writes Jane Pickard in *Personnel Management*. Their role, however, has completely changed. In place of allocating and checking on targets and rotas, the supervisor is now a facilitator and coach, encouraging the team to set up and measure its own systems. Teams, each with around ten members, are empowered to draw up rotas, organize their workload and provide ideas for improvements.

Although they have less direct supervision, teams still have tight guidelines to follow. At first these were oral and informal, but experience showed they needed to be formalized and written down. Ian Woolley, divisional director, consumer relations, worked out parameters with the teams to clarify what was expected in terms of output and internal relations. Written guidelines summarize company objectives and team targets. Terms of reference give more detail. For instance, consumer advisers are expected to be logged into the computer for 90 per cent of the time they are in the office, and on the phone for at least 55 per cent of the day. They can exceed targets, but if they fail to meet them, the team managers will discuss how they can improve.

The trickiest position in the new set-up is that of the ex-supervisor. Team manager Anne Marie Griffiths admits: 'The hardest thing was to hand over to someone else and trust them to do it as well as I would.'

Management attitudes can create barriers to teamworking. As Paul Neate, director of operations strategic development at Rothman's International, points out: 'What teams really require from managers is a commitment to allow them time to hold team meetings within working hours, when the more reactionary management would say that they should be producing the product.'

Many other companies, writes Pickard, including Rover and Vauxhall, have found that attitudes like these among supervisors create stumbling blocks to empowerment.

What role will support departments play?

The Work in America Institute recommends changing structures to make support people and experts directly available to teams.[11]

> Empowerment reshapes the relationships between supervisors and support staff. Employees need more advice in their expanded duties, supervisors have more time to seek it and, being empowered, team members should be free to seek support services themselves, and not have to go through the management hierarchy. As a result, it is often necessary to move staff nearer to the support staff, or make support staff part of the team.

This has been done at Walkers Smiths Snack Foods' Lincoln factory, where engineers have come out of the workshop and onto the factory floor. 'We used to work in a separate area but now we are each part of a production team,' says maintenance engineer Simon Aldous. 'Now that we are on the spot as part of the department we can respond more quickly to problems on the line. It also means we are working towards the same goals as the production team,' he says.

Adds engineer Wayne Clarke: 'One of the biggest changes for me this year has been being stationed in the plant and becoming part of the team there. It's a lot better – I really feel a sense of ownership of the equipment now, and there's much less downtime because I can respond more quickly.'

The factory has also done away with the demarcation line between production and packaging engineers and has trained all the engineers to do both jobs. 'Now any of them can work on any piece of equipment, anywhere in the factory,' says production engineer Gary Sharp. Lincoln's engineers have also taken on more management responsibility, he adds. 'We've cut out one layer of management, so engineers now report directly to production area managers, rather than through the maintenance manager. That makes the engineers' jobs much more responsible now.'

At Ciba, the Swiss multinational chemicals company, plant manager Colin McKay told the *Financial Times*: 'Previously, production people waited until something broke and the shit hit the fan. They then blamed the maintenance people, and the maintenance people blamed the production people for treating the machinery badly.'

Ciba's maintenance workers have now been incorporated

into the production team, helping production staff spot when machinery is likely to break down. Rather than running the plant to destruction, it can be shut down for half a day for preventive maintenance, saving three or four days' downtime. 'It sounds obvious, but it took time to change the habits of a lifetime,' says McKay.[12]

Support people also need both skill-based, multiskilling and teamwork training, says Wellins. 'Engineers, accountants and training people should be as skilled in team and interpersonal skills as are the team members themselves.'

What responsibilities will team leaders have?

'The key figure in the team is always the team leader,' says Rothman's Paul Neate. 'He or she is absolutely critical to the success of the team and it is therefore on this person that the greatest effort must be expended.'

Team leaders, according to management writers Bennis and Nanus, should, ideally, have the following characteristics:

❑ **vision:** knowing what they expect the team to be able to accomplish

❑ the ability to translate that vision into a set of meaningful goals for the team members

❑ **trust:** both trust in the members' capabilities, and the ability to earn the trust of the team members

❑ **self-management:** leaders must learn to manage themselves before they can hope to lead others.[13]

Unfortunately, as consultant Bernard Wynne has observed, many team leaders fall short of this ideal: 'Many team leaders, far from being part of the solution, are often part of the problem in teambuilding.'

Their weaknesses, he says, spring from a desire to maintain a higher status than the rest of the team, a lack of skill, and a desire to withhold information: 'In the early stages of team building, many teams find they need the help of an external facilitator – though not necessarily external to the company – to help them break down the barriers to team-working.'

Other organizations find spreading managerial tasks among several team members to be more effective, and more fitting with the idea of team work, than assigning a single leader. At Frizzell Financial Services, for example, besides a supervisor, each team also has a coordinator, who spends up to two hours a day representing and leading the team, a quality controller and someone to mastermind holidays, overtime and flexi-shifts. Many teams also have a sub-coordinator and a social events organizer. All five are elected and most teams rotate the positions about every three months between the most suitable and experienced people.

Do we need team leaders at all?

One British Rail train-cleaning crew at London Victoria station, who themselves had been hired to replace a group sacked for excessive absenteeism, approached their manager with complaints about their supervisor. They suggested they could do a better job on their own. The manager agreed, and the unsupervised team went on to substantially reduce absenteeism and improve productivity.

At W L Gore & Associates, a company that has become famous for its reliance on self-developing teams, there are no formal team leaders. Rather, according to Shipper and Manz, the various leadership functions are divided up among team members.

> W L Gore's is an alternative approach that promises to deliver many of the advantages and benefits of formally established empowered employee work teams – but without formally designated teams. Instead, the whole work operation becomes essentially one large empowered team in which everyone is individually self-managing and can interact directly with everyone else in the system. The company relies on self-developing teams without managers or bosses, but with lots of leaders.

An internal memo from W L Gore president Bill Gore describes how leadership roles in a team can be divided up among a number of individuals:

1. Some associates [all employees are called associates] are recognized by a team as having special knowledge or experience, for example a chemist, computer expert, salesperson, engineer or lawyer. This kind of leader gives the team guidance in a special area.

2. Some associates coordinate individual activities in order to achieve the agreed upon objectives of the team. His or her role is to persuade team members to make the commitments necessary for success.

3. Another associate (though often in practice the same individual who takes role no. 2) proposes necessary objectives and activities and seeks agreement and team consensus on objectives. This person is seen by the team as having a good grasp of how the objectives of the team fit in with the broad objectives of the enterprise.

4. Yet another associate takes charge of evaluating the relative contributions of team members and reporting these contributions to a renumeration committee.

Sherwood Computers, a London-based software house, turned its whole organization into 14 self-managing client teams. There are virtually no control services, with functions such as accounting incorporated into the teams. Each team has an annual budget and a three-year plan. Unless it gets into severe trouble, missing budgets badly, each team runs its own affairs without interference. Teams that are in trouble have a manager appointed temporarily. He or she may act in traditional directive style for a period, while the key problems are tackled, but more typically acts as an intensive coach, withdrawing once the team has recovered the confidence to manage its own affairs.

There are no official leaders, although about half of the teams have exercised their freedom to elect a small executive group. Top management at Sherwood is not entirely happy with this development. As chairman Bob Thomas told *The Times*:

As soon as there is even a semi-permanent group like that, the rest of the team can shuffle off responsibility and avoid the responsibility we want placed on, and accepted by, the whole team. We prefer the view that there are several leadership roles to be performed within a team and that rarely can one person fill them all.[14]

Brian Howes, Service and Industrial sector president for Europe at Kimberly Clark, has observed the evolution of a variety of self-managed team structures in his company's drive to empowerment. He explained to a conference in London:

> Should we appoint team leaders or should leadership rotate according to the subject under discussion?
>
> The answer may depend upon the stage of the teams' development and the maturity of the team members. Certainly as we have moved more towards self-appraisal we have recognized that some people continue to need much direction and coaching and I am now a supporter of the four stages of empowerment approach – with full empowerment being achieved only when the team members are judged to be competent. It sounds obvious but does not always happen in practice.

Rewarding team performance

According to Wellins,

> For years, American industry has rewarded the lone hero. Individual performance or seniority drove pay increases. But with a move toward self-directed teams, the attitudes toward compensation and reward systems have changed. Organizations using self-directed teams commonly implement various types of gain sharing or team bonus programs, along with skill based compensation plans.

Skill-based plans hold a unique advantage for self-directed teams because they reward team members for job depth, job breadth and vertical skills gained. Gain sharing or team bonus programmes can also reward team performance. These programs reward teams for increases in productivity that exceed some measure of baseline performance.

At Rogan Corporation in Northbrook, Illinois, for example,

team members reap bonuses when things go well, but share the pain when the company does poorly. In 1986 Rogan set up a gainsharing programme to lower its labour costs. The objective was to maintain labour costs as a percentage of the value of goods sold in a given week at 19.3 per cent. When fixed labour costs drop below that level, the difference goes to employees as a fifth monthly cheque. In 1992, the bonus yielded an extra 17 per cent of annual salaries.

Rogan teams have turned in more than 300 cost-cutting ideas since the programme's inception. Knowing that improvement will be shared fosters an allegiance to the company and closer attention to the entire work process. Moulder Lynette Bostic now keeps close tabs on the posted financial numbers: 'I look at the wall every morning to see what was shipped the day before,' she says. 'At the end of the week I can look at the board and see if we're ahead.'[15]

In many cases, management divides the bonus equally among team members, although occasionally teams decide how to distribute the bonus among themselves. At Dynavac Pty, in Melbourne Australia, employees have been setting each other's salaries since the 1970s. At Friedman's Microwave Oven Centers in Oakland California, president Arthur Friedman has given his teams complete freedom to decide for themselves how much they should earn and how much time off they should take. He also gave them access to the cash drawer, from which they could borrow money whenever they wanted, provided they left a debit note behind. If this sounds like a recipe for anarchy, Friedman says it generated so much goodwill among his employees that it paid off handsomely.[16]

ALTERNATIVE TEAM FORMATIONS

Self-directed teams are most commonly viewed as long-standing units of first-level employees – as the productive unit of the organization. Teams have, however, been used to good effect for other purposes, most notably as *ad hoc* problem-solving units, and as an alternative way to structure the management tiers.

Ad hoc first-level teams

Many companies use *ad hoc* teams to tackle one-off projects. These teams, made up of members drawn from various areas of the organization, can be very effective in tapping first-level skills and expertise. *Ad hoc* teams can offer:

❑ **Synergy:** the variety of backgrounds, abilities and viewpoints among members of *ad hoc* teams can often trigger ideas and solutions that might not arise within an ordinary work group.

❑ **Skills:** they can bring the abilities of front-line people to bear on problems and issues affecting the whole organization.

For example, when Walkers Smiths' marketing team wanted to improve and relaunch one of the company's flagship snack products, it gave the product improvement task not to the R & D department (though it too was involved) but directly to the shop floor operators who mixed, fried and packed the product.

'Investing in a relaunch meant we needed a top-quality product to go to market with, and the best people to help us make that happen were the operators themselves. After all, they work with the product day in and day out,' explains development manager Billy Brinkworth.

The product improvement project, called Quavers in Control, or QIC, involved about half the operators at the company's Lincoln plant. Each of the teams involved in the project had the support of quality assurance operatives and engineers, but were charged with finding improvements themselves.

'We divided the production process into eight areas and put a team of operators in charge of finding out what was needed to improve the output from each area,' says production engineer Gary Sharp.

And they were free to spend as much as they could justify on the project. One group spent £3,000 on a monitoring system to analyse the impact of the environment on the work in progress store. From that they discovered what was needed was a

£40,000 climatically controlled store. They presented their findings directly to the company's vice president of operations, and got the money.

So, while analysing production processes, seeking means of improving the product, running the numbers and preparing the presentation, all the team members were also actively involved in frying and packing the goods. Formal presentations were new to most of the workers, says cooker operator Kevan Robinson:

> I never thought I'd be doing this when I started here. A lot of the guys haven't done presentations before, and I can tell you – there are a few butterflies around here at the moment.
>
> I was surprised and pleased at the way the shop floor has been taken so seriously this time. Though not all of our ideas have been borne through, they were all taken seriously.

Robinson believes the company gained a lot from getting the shop floor involved.

> We've all got our own little areas of expertise, and by involving us and bringing those together, the company got a much better end result. For example, a lot of problems that would have had to be ironed out later were eliminated early on, because we know the machines and what problems might arise – an engineer might know what size part to use, but only an operator would know what it would catch on.

❑ **Motivation**: what better incentive to come up with new ideas than the knowledge that you may be able to implement them yourself?

At Ericsson General Electric, for example, employee teams, dubbed 'Win Teams', are given both the power and the budget to implement ideas they generate themselves. Membership of a Win Team is voluntary. Currently, there are 50 teams in the plant, each led by an elected line employee. A team has the authority to accept an idea, spend money on equipment to expedite the change, and implement it without management input. The budgetary limit for each team started out at $250 a year, but has since been increased to $6,000. Managers can belong to Win Teams, but only as resource people who do some of the interdepartmental legwork and research to see if an idea is feasible. Final approval and authority lie with the Win Team and its leader.[17]

Middle management teams

Middle management level teams tend to be either multi-disciplinary and issue-focused, or based on matrices – as when all the human resource or quality managers in a multi-site company meet together regularly to discuss policy, new techniques and common problems.

The main weakness of both these sorts of middle management teams is that they tend to be groups rather than empowered teams. They are rarely able to form a coherent work group with a common purpose – often because power is retained individually and only pooled under duress or in crisis.

At the executive level, teams often function as ancillaries to a strong chief executive, rather than as fully functioning teams in their own right. This can be a damaging situation because, if the top team is unable to present an example of effective teamwork, then it is unreasonable to expect others in the organization to do so.

Boards present an even greater problem. How do you make a team of a group of feisty individuals who only meet 12 times a year?

Members of executive teams need to:

❑ be able to stand in for each other on most aspects of directorships. They won't be expected to have in-depth functional expertise in all areas, but every director should be able to ask the right question of each major functional area

❑ have a common vision genuinely owned by all of them.

CONCLUSION

The idea of using teams as the basic unit of productivity in an organization is not new – Japanese car manufacturers have used them for decades. According to consultant Gillian

Laidlaw, Procter and Gamble were operating self-managed work teams as early as 1967, but they kept it a secret. 'They were performing so well they did not want any other company to have the same competitive advantage.'

What is new is the increasing role that self-managed teams are now playing in empowered organizations. Teamworking enables organizations to put a whole array of tasks and responsibilities in the hands of first-line people, whom it enables to take much more control over their work processes than they ever could as individuals. As such, teamworking is one of the most effective ways to help create an empowered organization.

According to Katzenbach and Smith of the McKinsey consultancy,

> teams will become the primary unit of performance in high performance organizations in the future. However, they will do so by enhancing or complementing, not totally crowding out, individual opportunity or formal hierarchy and process. Top management has to recognize the need to create and deploy them strategically.[18]

We will look at how both managers and individuals can complement the empowerment process in the following chapters.

References

1. Finegan, J., 'People power', *Inc*, July 1993.

2. Oates, D., 'Team players stretch ahead of the rest', *The Times*, 27 May 1993.

3. Bluestone, B., and Bluestone, I., 'Workers (and managers) of the world unite', *Technology Review*, November/December 1992.

4. Ibid.

5. Wellins, R., 'Building self directed teams', *Technical and Skills Training*', May/June 1992.

6. Seath, I. and Clark, J., 'A clean-cut vision of progression', *Managing Service Quality*, November 1993.

7. Baxter, A., 'Selectors choice', *Financial Times*, 11 August 1993.

8. Shipper, F. and Manz, C., 'An alternative road to empowerment', *Organizational Dynamics*, June 1990.

9. De Jonquieres, G., 'A clean break with tradition', *Financial Times*, 12 July 1993.

10. Pickard, J., 'The real meaning of empowerment', *Personnel Management*, November 1993.

11. 'New roles for managers', Work in America Institute Inc, Scarsdale, NY, 1991.

12. Abrams, P, 'Creating cracks in the layers', *Financial Times*, 5 April 1993.

13. Bennis, W. G., and Nanus B, (1985), *Leaders; a Strategy for Taking Charge*, London.

14. Oates, D., 'Team players stretch ahead of the rest', op. cit.

15. Ehrenfeld, T., 'Cashing in', *Inc*, July 1993.

16. Handy, C. (1984), *The Remaking of Work*, Blackwells, Oxford.

17. Filipczak, R., 'Ericsson General Electric, the evolution of empowerment', *Training*, September 1993.

18. Katzenbach, J. A. and Smith, D. K., 'The discipline of teams', *Harvard Business Review*, March–April, 1993.

5
CHANGING THE BEHAVIOUR OF MANAGERS

This fad of empowerment... what companies mean by it varies dramatically. Many of them are really talking about firing middle management.
Peter Senge, MIT Sloane School of Management.

Oddly enough, it's managers who are having the toughest time making the shift. Well, it's not so odd, on second thought. Many of their jobs are disappearing.
Tom Peters, author and consultant.

We have a layer of clay that prevents anything going either way – up or down. That layer is middle management.
Ciba chief operating officer Heini Lippuner.

Many managers plotted, sweated and sacrificed for years to acquire the power and authority they possess. Now they're supposed to give it up without a fight?
Peter Kizilos, management writer.

Managers at all levels will readily acknowledge the benefits of empowering their workforce. Most will just as readily resist it.

Empowering is a very difficult thing for managers to do. Not only does it run counter to everything they've been trained to do and everything they've worked for, in many cases it represents a direct threat to their jobs – or certainly to their jobs as they know them.

For some the prospect is out and out frightening, says Gavin Barrett, MD of Sundridge Park Management Centre in London: 'When the question is put to executives in public and corporate development programmes: "How many of you know managers who have a mortal dread of excellence in their subordinates?", the response is overwhelmingly depressing.'

As one food factory operator observed: 'Managers don't really want to let go. As soon as you take control, they put their power hat back on.' There are various reasons for this, including:

❑ **Habit:** according to author William Byham,

> Empowerment is really hard for supervisors and managers because all their lives they've been trained to make decisions and solve problems for people. Now you're asking them to do something that is very different – to be a coach to people, to help them solve their own problems. To training people that sounds like a natural thing to do, but it is an extremely diffi-cult thing for a [line] manager.[1]

Robert Frey, owner and president of Cine-Made, a Cincinnati can manufacturer, discovered this when he tried to empower his workforce:

> My managers felt they were paid to be worthy adversaries of the unions. It's what they'd been trained for. It's what made them good managers. Moreover, they were not used to partici-pation in any form; certainly not in decision-making. One of them devised at least a dozen ways of de-laying and obstruct-ing the flow of necessary numbers to the employees. As for profit sharing, another of my managers declared it to be a form of communism.[2]

❑ **Fear of anarchy:** the ambivalence that many managers feel about the concept of empowerment is exemplified by research undertaken recently among the top managers of ten large British companies by Laurie International, a management consultancy.

> These leaders all agreed that empowerment was vital to the improvement of business efficiency and quality, but they detected worry among their managers 'that empowerment could open up a Pandora's box'. Many of the managers feared empowerment's potential for anarchy and many were emphat-ic 'that empowerment boundaries would have to be set'.[3]

❑ **Personal insecurity:** in an empowered organization, many managers find they are asked to manage people who have more technical or professional skills than they do. The prospect can be a daunting one.

Coverdale consultant Milo Lynch has seen managers frightened by too much employee initiative:

In an empowered organization, you want to generate so much confidence that people are constantly pushing at their manager. But you have to be careful of going too far too fast. In one plant I worked in, the operators were so highly enthused and coming up with so many ideas that the managers became frightened and stifled the initiative.

In a large food distributor, persuading employees to take greater responsibility for quality and customer care issues was central to the business strategy. But the operations director, an outwardly strong individual with a core team of like-minded managers around him, effectively sabotaged the strategy by regarding every suggestion from below as a direct criticism of him and his managers. The removal of this person and some of his colleagues was like opening a bottle of shaken sparkling wine. Once the realization that ideas were now welcome had sunk in, an explosion of suggestions occurred.

❑ **Lack of skills:** empowerment asks managers to harness subordinate talent while maintaining enough control to maximize efficiency. This is an exacting task, and not one to ask of managers without offering training and support.

And, as Milo Lynch discovered, few managers are recruited for their ability to empower staff, or given training in it once on the job.

Many manufacturing companies I have worked with tend to employ technical graduates who have been recruited because they are competent and intelligent. The management style they often evolve is one of constantly giving instructions to their subordinates and not allowing scope for participation. The organization itself will devise top-down strategies which deny participation from the workforce. It may well be that UK industry is informed by military service models as the style it unconsciously emulates. Or to put it another way, employees are treated as children.

❑ **Pragmatism:** empowerment doesn't solve everything, or work in every situation. In some circumstances, it may be inappropriate, undesirable or impossible, and managers recognize this.

'Most of us can recall instances in which such practices as the threat of punishment increased our motivation to comply with a supervisor's expectations. That phenomenon holds true in the boardroom as well as on the shop floor,' says William Kahnweiler, an assistant professor of human resources development at Georgia State University. 'Throw in tight deadlines, irate customers and the need for quick decisions, and you have the recipe for autocratic rule. When our backs are against the wall, we're more likely to respond with immediate, direct action than with attempts to empower others.'[4]

This phenomenon can be seen with particular clarity in a turnaround situation. When the company is deep in crisis the overwhelming need expressed by the individuals and teams in the organization is often for:

❑ strong, directive leadership

❑ visible, positive action, even if this has painful side-effects, such as job losses or the termination of pet projects,

❑ a clear sense of purpose.

Achieving these by consensus takes too long, gives an opportunity for individual interest groups to take political positions and is likely to result in dangerous half-measures that delay recovery.

However, consensus is not empowerment. Properly managed, empowerment can be a major support of turnaround. The key is to define precisely *where* and *what* to ask people to take responsibility for and seriously to recognize that many of the problems the organization faces are at least partially a result of a failure to empower.

Top management needs to define strategy and critical control processes. How the strategy is achieved within those controls needs to be left to the discretion of the managers and operating teams.

If each management layer of the organization does not pass down accountability and responsibility, then it delays recovery just as effectively as would have been the case through consensus. Effective turnaround requires a clear focus on the priorities by all the key people. That simply isn't possible if they are doing part or all of someone else's job.

Exactly how to define the appropriate level of responsibility and, even more difficult, how to persuade people to accept and respond to the challenge, are themes for later chapters. Suffice to say that the role of the turnaround manager is in large part one of persuasion and stimulation of all the teams in the organization, rather than just the development and administration of a survival strategy.

❑ **Lack of top management example:** why, middle managers quite reasonably ask, should I take the risk of letting my people make more decisions when my own boss still runs his department as if by divine right?

❑ **Job and promotion insecurity:** as organizations flatten and front-line people take on more responsibility, managers, particularly middle managers, tend to be the ones that go. According to *The Employment Gazette*, 35,000 British middle managers were made redundant in the first half of 1992. The survivors worry, with some justification, that they are fast becoming an endangered species.

Even managers who are under no threat of redundancy may resent empowerment's implied threat to the organizational power which they have worked so hard to attain. According to John Burdett, vice-president of the Canadian packaging conglomerate, the Lawson Mardon Group: 'The traditional approach to power assumes that if someone gets more power, someone else must lose power. It is exactly this notion and the insecurity behind it that prevents many executives, and often those at senior levels, from encouraging and supporting employee involvement initiatives.'[5]

Graham Oddey, an executive consultant with KPMG Peat Marwick, once encountered an unusual middle manager:

He said: 'My job is to work myself out of a job by empowering my staff.' He was confident that if he adopted this approach, his employers, far from seizing the chance to get rid of him, would value him all the more and find him another job. As things turned out, his confidence was well-founded.[6]

But does empowerment necessarily threaten the very existence of managers and supervisors? The answer is no. In fact, they are needed more than ever in an empowered organization. Their role, however, must change dramatically. Once the empowered employee is able to assume 'managerial' functions such as controlling and scheduling work, appraising and disciplining other team members and taking responsibility for the quality of the finished product or service, managers are free to take on an entirely new set of responsibilities. These may include coaching and training team members, helping employees find the resources they need, or helping the team coordinate its efforts with other parts of the organization.

At Harvester Restaurants, for example, everyone, including waitresses, cooks and bar staff, has one or more managerial responsibilities, called accountabilities, which include recruitment, drawing up rotas and keeping track of sales targets in the restaurant. These are not allocated by the manager, but shared among staff at their weekly team meetings.

This, it would seem, would leave very little for the branch manager to do, but, as branch manager Bernard O'Neill says: 'My role is now mainly one of marketing. I am spending much more time going out into the community getting business.' He has also had to act as a facilitator, encouraging people to believe they can organize themselves in such a new way.[7]

Managers in empowered organizations in any industry must take on a number of new roles.

Counsellor or coach

At all levels, the empowering relationship is rather like learning to drive. At a critical point, the novice driver goes solo. The instructor has to accept that he or she is no longer in control. Management writer David Oates draws a sporting analogy:

A sports coach will devote plenty of effort to preparing a team for match day, but, once the game is under way, he is confined to the sidelines. Only the players can execute the game plan. Similarly, empowering managers coach their employees for the task in hand and then leave them to get on with it. As David Whitaker, who coached the English hockey team to a gold medal at the Seoul Olympics, puts it: 'It's a big challenge for business managers to enable their subordinates to do a better job than they could probably do, but it's absolutely critical in coaching.'[8]

It is essential too, adds consultant Rob Gordon, that managers help the people working for them to learn from experience: 'This process is crucial to the effectiveness of empowered teams and individuals; and the manager has a leading role in ensuring it happens.'

The empowering manager must become a counsellor to the team and the individuals in it. This counselling should not primarily be concerned with solving problems or seeking particular answers; rather it should aim to help people understand more clearly how they are managing a situation, how they make things easy or difficult for themselves, and how they might be restricting their ability to solve problems. Answers to problems should emerge during counselling, but the impetus for the solution should come from the employee. It is not the manager's job to suggest answers but to facilitate the employee's understanding of the situation and his or her own solving of the problem.

As William Byham points out, employees will come to their managers with poor ideas.

> You can handle them in such a way that they will never come back to you with another idea. The ideal response is always 'try it out and learn from it'. But you just can't let that happen every time. Instead you have to encourage them to come up with another, better idea.
>
> One of the big challenges is teaching managers how to use control properly, how to use it in such a way that it does not sap people.[9]

Articulator of vision

If people share a common set of goals and a common perspective on what to do and how to accomplish it, they are able to work without waiting for orders. The manager's task, then, is not to give orders, but to articulate this common set of goals or vision and to encourage employees to share it.

Fewer things can be more difficult than getting others to share a dream and managers can only expect to achieve this if they themselves genuinely believe in the ideals they want their employees to aspire to, living by them and talking about them openly.

Goal definer

The manager should define the team's goals clearly and give constant performance feedback. Instead of giving instructions, he or she should agree targets and then let the team or individual decide how best to meet them.

It is important for the manager only to intervene in *how* the job is done either when the employee asks for help or when disaster is otherwise inevitable. Every time the manager has to intervene without being asked, it diminishes the employee's self-esteem and willingness to take initiative in the future. Learning how to walk this tightrope is perhaps the toughest element of empowerment for many managers.

Creator of challenge

The manager is often the team's spokesperson. If challenging activities are on offer, then he should make sure his employees get a fair chance to do them by marketing their skills to the rest of the company. If there are no challenges in the offing, the manager's task is to set about creating some.

Developer of talent

The manager tracks the employee's progress and provides help and encouragement. He or she takes a personal interest in developing employees' careers by ensuring they are aware of opportunities and inspiring him or her to take them up. Although the role of mentor is normally an off-line relationship, in an empowered team, it becomes much easier for the manager to adopt mentoring behaviours.

Resource obtainer

Empowering managers see their task as ensuring that resources, whether they be supplies, educational opportunities or adherence to the latest health and safety legislation, are available when the team needs them; and, instead of using hierarchy to get things done, put their efforts into removing obstacles that might keep their people from getting things done.

The role is what management writer Robert K Greenleaf called servant-leaders. According to John Carlson, vice president of TU Electric in Dallas, Texas: 'Servant leadership is helping your subordinates to be successful and doing it anonymously. You don't qualify as a servant leader if you share with the subordinates all you've done to help them be successful or accomplish a certain task.'

Adds Michael Murray of Creative Interchange Consultants in Arlington, Texas:

> Instead of thinking about what they can do for you, think about what you can do for them. Then go to your boss and get it settled that one of your goals is how you can help the Carol, Charlie and Bob, who report to you, do better this year. Have it understood that your success should be measured by their growth.[10]

Leader

For the manager, releasing control does not necessarily mean releasing responsibility. He has to find new ways to influence people so that they use their new freedoms wisely. He or she also remains accountable to the organization for the overall performance of the empowered team.

This is best accomplished by a gradual change – particularly if the manager's starting point is a dictatorial leadership style. The manager should first explain what he is going to do, sell the benefits to the workforce, then coach staff how to take on the new responsibilities. An enabling period follows, where the employees are given the chance to exercise their new roles under supervision, gradually extending their control as they gain confidence and expertise. Only after this gradual process has taken place can employees be empowered. The schematic picture of the process will look like this: telling – selling – coaching – enabling – empowering.

Telling and selling styles tend to belong to *controlling* leaders, who attempt to make people perform by either directing or manipulating them. Coaching and enabling styles are used by *enabling* leaders, who perceive that greater value will accrue from giving people the confidence and competence to make their own decisions, but who nonetheless remain in the background to pick up the pieces, correct mistakes and provide a backstop. *Empowering* leaders perceive their role as a resource available to help the team at its own request.

Controlling leaders

❑ select the right product

❑ select the right employees

❑ define processes, procedures and standards

❑ set objectives and guidelines.

Enabling leaders

❑ encourage cross-training

❑ appraise performance continuously

❑ promote communication between their department and other departments, suppliers and relevant organizations

❑ build and nurture the team

❑ encourage employees to take up training and education opportunities.

Empowering leaders

❏ coordinate direction (in the sense of where are we going?)

❏ procure resources (money, equipment, knowledge and expertise)

❏ are available when needed

❏ represent the team when needed (with the team's consent – in many cases they may prefer one of their own members to make presentations).

Leadership in an empowered organization calls for dramatic changes in role, approach and appraisal systems at each of supervisory, middle management and executive levels. We will look at each in turn.

The supervisor

Walking the line between management and shop floor, supervisors are ideally placed to be agents of change. They are equally well-placed to block it – something that firms often fail to anticipate.

According to a recent Confederation of British Industry (CBI) report:[11] 'The potential among supervisors exists, but is not being harnessed. It is a resource which is currently being ignored, under-utilized and demotivated. We need trained, skilled supervisors whose role is clear, whose contribution is valued and whose motivation is assured.'

In a study of engineering and textile plants in Britain, France and Germany, the CBI found that, in Germany, line supervisors were aware of their section's production costs and received production schedules well in advance for forward planning. They were also paid about 40 per cent more than the average skilled worker. In the UK, this difference is about 20 per cent.

In Britain, according to the report, supervisors frequently face crisis management – chasing supplies, rescheduling because of breakdowns, and training new staff because of high turnover. Companies, such as Nissan, which pay their supervisors salary levels equal to those of professional engineers and other equivalent postings, are rare.

Much is asked of supervisors anyway. More is expected after an empowerment initiative, and many find the change to be stressful, challenging, and threatening to their power and security. They are neither part of management, nor are they members of the workforce. Yet, because they are seen to be part of management, their commitment and enthusiasm for the change tends to be taken for granted. Companies put a lot of effort into winning the acceptance of the shop floor, and almost none into carrying along those who supervise them.

The role of supervisor needs to shift from controller, to motivator, planner and enabler. This is not an easy adjustment for many front-line supervisors to make. Many reached management positions on the basis of their technical competence, not because of their motivation to lead and manage others. Some may not want to make the change and will prefer to return to team member positions or to become technical experts in a particular skill or process, rather than team facilitators and coaches.

A report from the Work in America Institute[12] advises how to help supervisors make the transition from being a supervisor relying mainly on operational skills to a team leader using primarily management skills:

❑ Ensure that managers and supervisors play an active part in deciding the goals and parameters of employee involvement and the plan for implementing it.

❑ Clarify the supervisors' role. Are they front-line managers or team leaders? Are they responsible for the performance of the empowered team? Titles such as 'coordinator' or 'advisor' suggest not, but in practice if anything goes wrong, the supervisor answers for it. So, where supervisors are responsible for team performance, call them managers, train them, and even better, pay them as such.

❑ As workers become more self-directing, encourage supervisors to expand their roles.

At Buckingham Foods, part of the Booker Food Group, the management team realized that if other shopfloor reforms were to succeed, the role of supervisor had to be addressed.

'I'd describe myself as a middle manager,' says Sharon Roy, a supervisor at Buckingham Foods:

> I make my own decisions about how I achieve the production targets and I am responsible for quality control. Before, I used to come in and pick up a sheet which said how many sandwiches we had to produce and what variety. I had no influence on the number of staff required on a line, any input into how long processes should take, or any direct control over the machinery.
>
> Things have changed. If the line breaks down now, I don't just report it to my superior like I used to do. Rather, I have the authority to get hold of the engineer to get the work done.
>
> I have production targets and I want to meet them.

Supervisors at Buckingham attend regular off-the-job training sessions. Says factory manager Tony Pritchard: 'These not only enhance individuals' skills but send very clear signals to the workforce that supervisors are important.'[13]

Michelin Tyre's group personnel manager Bob Bell describes a similar change in his organization:

> Within Michelin UK the change which we asked of our foremen was directly related to our business need. Before introducing empowerment in 1980, we had depended on inspecting in quality with its inherent costs. The foreman's role was task-oriented with a heavy emphasis on chasing the progress of work. Shopfloor employees were paid on an incentive scheme that ensured volume of production, and sophisticated inspection techniques guaranteed final product quality to the customer.
>
> By 1980, however, it was obvious that increased costs of both raw materials and manpower called for a different approach if Michelin was to continue to compete on quality and cost. To do this, the way we managed employees and our expectations of what they could contribute had to change.
>
> We never envisaged at the outset the potential of our workforce that this would release.
>
> Rather than launching into a full-fledged empowerment programme, however, we initially piloted a number of related initiatives, including quality circles, redefinition of training

and validation, performance reviews for shopfloor employees, multiskilling of engineers, post development of production employees, team meetings and statistical process control.

The piloting exercises helped us to recognize the strength of certain approaches and to learn from our mistakes. One such mistake was to implement mass training rather than designing training which balances the needs of the individual with the requirements of the business.

All the pilot programmes included elements of empowerment for the employees and thus had a direct impact on the foremen's relationships with shopfloor employees. Now they needed to encourage and involve employees, and to evaluate, through performance reviews, how the employees did their jobs.

The biggest change, however, was to redefine the role of foreman to that of shift manager, then train and counsel them to be managers who could orchestrate, rather than direct, their human resources. We expected them to create and maintain an environment in which effective working relationships could flourish, and to work with all employees to develop competence in their role, commitment to local objectives and capacity for change.

Bell outlines how the roles have changed:

From foreman	*To shift manager*
Get results primarily by directing people and getting their cooperation	Involve people and help them invest their personal commitment
Build good followers	Build good initiators
Get people to understand good ideas	Get people to generate good ideas
Manage people one on one	Build collaborative, interdependent, and supportive teams
Develop strength within your own unit	Develop strength between our unit, other units and your peers
Implement directions from above	Initiate new ideas and directions yourself at your own level.

| Help people change when directed and help them make the best of it | Generate positive innovations with your people without those changes being imposed from above |
| Communicate well | Be masterful at interpersonal communications. |

Middle managers

As supervisors take on more managerial tasks, what is left for the middle manager to do? asks Paul Neate, director of operations strategic development at Rothman's International in a speech to an IIR seminar in November 1992: 'The very fact of developing a cadre of well trained, highly motivated managers at the existing supervisory level will inevitably diminish the pivotal role of the middle manager. Indeed, in many cases, if not all, the position of middle manager will disappear – or at best, will be radically changed.'

No wonder, then, that middle management is often cited as the most obstinate barrier to empowerment in an organization. After all, as Tom Peters points out, it is their jobs which are disappearing.[14] Yet, argues Neate, middle managers play a crucial role in encouraging supervisors to enable their teams, use new skills and accept responsibility and accountability:

> The whole structure of the traditional organisation moves around the middle manager. He or she is charged with communicating top management decisions, implementing those decisions and amending them so that the often ill-conceived dreams of the board are converted into what is practical on the shop floor. And he does this through a supervisory corps which is typically well-educated in process disciplines but woefully inadequate in people management skills, and is in any case unsure of his position and authority.
>
> So after an empowerment initiative, there will still be middle managers. There will just be fewer of them. Their role will be across several disciplines but not in such detail. They will be coordinators; they will have fewer direct reports but cover a wider scope of activity.

With a wider span of activity, however, there is a risk that some middle managers may drift too far from the coal-face. As one food factory supervisor noted: 'Some managers, because they have less reason to get involved in the day to day running of things, lose touch with the shop floor and start to manage by figures and reports.'

To win middle management support for an empowerment initiative, Neate advises:

❑ Involve them in the shape of the new organization, and be completely honest with them about it. The new – and fewer – positions must be clearly shown from the beginning and the span of management must be clearly defined.

❑ As part of the selection process, carry out a management skills inventory to identify not only the assets available among the existing middle management corps, but also the gaps which have to be filled.

❑ In selecting management, their functional skills – accountancy, engineering, etc. – must be only the base-building blocks and almost taken for granted. The real skills of the manager – delegation, counselling, facilitating and communications – must be grafted on to the base discipline and become the main task, rather than something casually picked up along the way.

❑ Don't even attempt empowerment without the commitment of senior management. 'This is so vital that no organizational change can, or should ever, be attempted without it,' he says.

Everyone has seen or experienced personally individual managers returning from a course or seminar fired up with enthusiasm, and immediately attempting to put into practice the new ideas he or she has learned, only to come up against opposition from above and apathy from below. The inevitable result is frustration and disillusionment, perhaps even greater than before.

This happened at Ciba, the pharmaceutical firm: 'The critical area [in empowerment] is middle management. If it stops there then the whole exercise is wasted. Some fully support the changes, while others are afraid, while others refuse to delegate because they believe that by doing so they lose power,' says Ciba Chairman Alex Krauer. Adds Ciba chief operating officer Heini Lippuner:

> I meet young people on the shop floor who tell me they like the vision [Ciba's change programme, Vision 2000] and believe we are sincere about empowerment. But they complain there has been no real change. To put it pointedly, it looks as though we have a layer of clay that prevents anything going either way – up or down. That layer is middle management.

Ciba senior management plan to crack the layer of clay by creating pressure from both above and below, and through education. Questionnaires were sent to the 20,000 employees in Switzerland about their managers' leadership behaviour. The aim, says Krauer, was to set up a level of expectation from employees and use that expectation to force middle managers into dialogue.

Krauer believes 90 per cent of managers are capable of adopting the vision. 'A few, and I hope only a few, will not want to cooperate and they had better look for a job outside Ciba,' he says. 'There's too much at stake for people in key positions not to be part of the process.'[15]

Executives

For middle managers to work effectively, senior management has to let go of much of its leadership role. Although ultimately the executive team or the board can overrule any decision, middle managers need to feel that, in practice, the organization has such confidence in them and in its basic systems that the ultimate authority to decide matters that concern their job is either theirs alone, or is shared with their colleagues.

Executives, too, need to be empowered. As Chris Hughes, general manager at Whitbread's Magor Brewery, says:

> Much of our expertise was concentrated in a highly experienced upper management team which took responsibility for the day-to-day running of the brewery. But the jobs at the top

in this industry have become bigger, more strategy oriented, and they now require a greater commitment to developing far-sighted policies far from the distractions of incessant operational queries.

Empowerment demands a whole new set of behaviours, which have to be cascaded down the management structure. It starts with having a board that actually thinks and behaves like a board. Instead of concerning itself with a multitude of operational activities, the board confines itself to the strategic issues, which are the essence of effective direction. In doing so, it empowers the executive team to focus on making the strategy happen.

It then becomes much easier to delegate responsibility and authority to senior managers, on the basis of 'What is the lowest point in the organization at which this decision can effectively be made?' There then begins a lengthy process of self-education and of educating direct reports into accepting and using delegated authority, and into how to adopt similar behaviours towards their own direct reports.

Top managers' approach to power will also have to change dramatically. Most senior executives did not get where they are by empowering others; empowering traits have not traditionally been valued on the fast track to the board room. Even now, empowering traits do not figure much in selecting the leaders of the future.

Research by Dr Lynda Gratton of the London Business School into fast tracking – the process by which companies turn talented young managers quickly into the high-powered elite – found that 'the values and behaviour patterns which they promote among today's star middle managers and tomorrow's top dogs are in direct conflict with the concept of empowerment.'

Gratton looked at how well high fliers used the various behaviours that can be considered empowering and whether they gave these any priority. The answer, in most cases, was negative. The top strengths to emerge in the study were individual rather than team ones. The 100 managers studied were seen by themselves and their subordinates as highly energetic, hard-working, analytically able, action-oriented and intelligent. Yet most were seen to be weak on half of the

20 categories of empowerment, and not very strong on any. In particular, 42 per cent were described as expecting too much of, and being impatient towards, people with different abilities and needs. A recurrent phrase was: 'does not suffer fools gladly'.

'It is not surprising that high fliers tend to manage very much in their boss's image, but if an organization is really serious about empowerment,' says Gratton, 'it must revamp its processes for developing leaders'. Companies should, she recommends, select individuals for the fast track only after their delegation and team-building potential has been assessed in action, and allow entry to fast tracks at several stages in people's careers.[16]

If the fast track is not setting an example to future executives, who is? Female top managers, apparently. According to Judy B. Rosener, a faculty member at the Graduate School of Management at the University of California: 'Women who have broken the glass ceiling in medium-sized non traditional organizations have demonstrated that using the command and control style of managing others is not the only way to succeed.'

In a study sponsored by the International Women's Forum,[17] Rosener found that many of the management approaches typically used by executive women bear a remarkable similarity to those considered empowering:

> Men are more likely than women to describe their managerial style along the lines of transactional leadership. That is, as a series of transactions with subordinates – exchanging rewards for services rendered or punishment for inadequate performance. The men are also more likely to use power that comes from their organizational position and formal authority. The women respondents, on the other hand, described themselves in ways that characterize 'transformational' leadership – getting subordinates to transform their own self interest into the interest of the group through concern for a broader goal. They are also more likely than men to use power based on personal characteristics like charisma, interpersonal skills, hard work, or contacts, rather than that based on organizational position, title and the ability to reward or punish.

The women leaders made frequent reference to their efforts

to encourage participation and share power and information – two things that are often associated with empowerment. They also described attempts to enhance other people's self-worth and to energize followers. In general, these leaders believe that people perform best when they feel good about themselves and their work, and they try to create situations that contribute to that feeling. All of which point to an empowering management style.

MEASURING THE SUCCESS OF MANAGERS

A critical step in developing empowered and empowering managers is to turn the appraisal system on its head. All managers should be rewarded for their ability to release the potential of their subordinates in measurable terms; and appraisal and evaluation should be done not just by the boss, and not just on short-term performance, but over the long term, by colleagues and subordinates as well. This is what is known as '360 degree feedback' – an assessment of performance for superiors, colleagues, and, most importantly, subordinates.

There are a number of advantages to this system (which originated in Leningrad (St Petersburg) in the early 1970s) for both managers and subordinates, says Adrian Furnham, head of University College London's Business Psychology Unit:

❑ Subordinates tend to know their superiors better than superiors know their subordinates.

❑ There are generally more subordinates than superiors, so subordinates' ratings can give a more accurate statistical picture of managers' performance.

❑ Subordinates' ratings have more impact because it is more unusual to receive ratings from subordinates.

There are also, he adds, a number of dangers to upward appraisal:

❑ Some employees might hesitate to give a frank and fair appraisal of their boss for fear of reprisal.

❑ Some may be unused to giving any kind of feedback and veer towards the bland, and uninformative, middle of the scale.

❑ An opportunity to give anonymous ratings might lead some employees to be vindictive.

❑ There are greater costs involved. Paperwork, software and the training to use them all cost money.[18]

The practice of 360 degree appraisal is, according to consultant Graham Oddey, still not widespread:

> It is rare to find measures [of management effectiveness] associated in any meaningful way with how well they empower their people, yet it need not be too hard to change this. For instance, try measuring employees' views of how well their managers motivate them, how helpful they are, or how much their managers trust them, and feed these into the managers' appraisals. You could also think about measures of employee activity, such as the number of suggestions put forward per employee, and the percentage which are implemented. Measure managers, as well as employees, on absenteeism levels. Ask employees whether they would recommend your company to others as a place to work, and measure managers on the trend in responses as empowerment takes hold.[19]

Companies that practise 360 degree appraisals include Motorola, Semco Brazil, British Petroleum, British Airways, Central Television, Cathay Pacific and Peritas.

At Motorola, appraisal by subordinates as well as superiors not only makes managers more aware of the skills they require as bosses, but ensures that the process of appraisal (which is important because of performance-related pay) is regarded as fairer and more objective.[20]

Semco Brazil's upward appraisal system is engrained in its culture. Management appraisal at this Sao Paulo-based paragon of empowerment now involves more than 30 questions and takes place twice a year. A score of 80 per cent is average. Those people who regularly underperform tend to leave. Chief executive – or, as he prefers to be known, counsellor – Ricardo Semler's latest score was 82 per cent.[21]

At Ciba UK, the training department has sampled workforce opinion to find out how empowering their managers are. Managers and their subordinates were asked to rate individual managers on such dimensions as 'ensures openness,' 'promotes cooperation,' 'delegates authority' and 'develops people'. The subordinates' views were slightly less flattering than the subjects' own, but between the first survey in 1991 and the second in 1992, ratings improved significantly. The training department is encouraged, and the management team believes the survey is a useful way of measuring the general climate of opinion over the long term.[22]

Peritas, an autonomous consultancy and training business owned by ICL, launched a 360 degree appraisal system in the spring of 1994. 'Many management teams convince themselves that they're managing in a particular way and are perceived in a particular way, but when they conduct a 360 degree appraisal they get a serious dose of reality,' says Peritas executive chairman David Wimpress.

The company's 1993 employee opinion survey results supported what Wimpress had already identified: a need to change the culture of the business; to empower middle manager and service staff to drive the changes; and to make Peritas a more exciting and vibrant place in which to work.

The plan, says Wimpress, is to have all 250 staff in the business appraise the managers immediately above them. Managers can then develop personal action plans in the light of the feedback they get. They are also expected to be completely open about the results – Peritas managers will inform staff of the results of their own appraisals as part of each subordinate's appraisal.

The initiative has already had a powerful effect on staff attitudes. 'At the first three staff briefings I held, people were very passive,' says Wimpress:

> I had to tell them I was prepared to stand there as long as it took to get a dialogue going. But when they were told about the new appraisal system, there was an immediate buzz in the room. There was a great deal of discussion and debate and we even got a round of applause. There was only one negative question, and that was fielded by an employee on the floor. It's signs like this that tell you the spirit of an organization really is changing.

Not everyone was keen at first, though. Some managers did have misgivings, though they came round when reminded that they were also empowered to implement the new system, explains Wimpress.

Three hundred and sixty degree appraisals are part of Peritas' 'truth to power' drive:

> We want to develop a culture where people within the company feel comfortable telling the truth to the powerful. Otherwise, managers in charge of driving change will never find out what they really need to know. If the emperor is wearing no clothes, people must be free to tell him so.

CONCLUSION

Empowerment can be a frightening prospect for managers at all levels. But if they worry about their job security and satisfaction in an empowered organization, they may have more to worry about in an unempowered one. Not only are empowered organizations arguably more competitive, and thus more likely to survive in the long term, but the job of a manager in an empowered organization can be immensely more satisfying than in a comparable command and control role.

Instead of playing policemen, empowering managers can share ideas with and learn from their employees. They are also freed of much of the rote work involved in running the company, and thus themselves empowered to get on with the job of strategy formulation, planning and leadership. As Robert Frey, CEO of Cine Made Corporation, said of his company's empowerment initiative: 'If it worked, we'd all be better off. If nothing else, I'd sleep better at night from not feeling so damned lonely.'[23]

References

1. Kizilos, P., 'Crazy about empowerment', *Training*, December 1990.

2. Frey, R., 'Empowerment or else', *Harvard Business Review*, September-October 1993.

3. Lorenz, C., 'Making fast tracks more empowering', *Financial Times*, 8 July 1992.

4. Kahnweiler, W.M., 'HRD and empowerment', *Training and Development*, November 1991.

5. Burdett, J.O., 'What is empowerment anyway?' *Journal of European Industrial Training*, Vol 15, no 6, 1991.

6. Oddey, G., 'Take a horse to water, but ...' *Managing Service Quality*, November 1993.

7. Pickard, J., 'The real meaning of empowerment', *Personnel Management*, November 1993.

8. Oates, D., 'Coaching staff to beat the opposition', *The Times*, 23 September 1993.

9. Kizilos, P., 'Crazy about empowerment', op. cit.

10. Greenleaf, R.K., Management letter, Bureau of Business Practice, Waterford Connecticut.

11. Wood, L., 'Profit by power to the middle manager', *Financial Times*, 5 January 1993.

12. *New Roles for Managers*, The Work in America Institute Inc: Scarsdale NY, 1991.

13. Wood, L., 'Profit by power to the middle manager', op. cit.

14. Peters, T., 'Crazy Ways for Crazy Days', BBC2, 6 December 1993.

15. Abrahams, P., 'Creating cracks in the layers', *Financial Times*, 5 April 1993.

16. Lorenz, C., 'Making fast tracks more empowering' op. cit.

17. Rosener, J.B., 'Ways women lead', *Harvard Business Review*, November/December 1990.

18. Furnham, A., 'When employees rate their superiors', *Financial Times*, 1 March 1993.

19. Oddey, G., 'Take a horse to water, but ...' op. cit.

20. Barry, T., 'Empowerment, the new practice in personnel management', *Multinational Employer*, May 1991.

21. Hall, E., 'The boss from Brazil', *Personnel Today*; 26 October 1993.

22. Pickard, J., 'The real meaning of empowerment', op. cit.

23. Frey, R., 'Empowerment or else', op. cit.

6
CHANGING THE BEHAVIOUR OF INDIVIDUALS

What did it cost? Just our brain power.

Walkers Smiths fryer operator

The idea that to make a man work you've got to hold gold in front of his eyes is a growth, not an axiom. We've done that for so long that we've forgotten there's any other way.

F. Scott Fitzgerald.

It doesn't matter whose name is on the gate, because this is my company.

Jimmy Howerton, an associate at Ericsson GE

One of the more interesting linguistic comparisons in company literature is the way companies talk about their empowerment programmes. Does the language imply that people are considered primarily *en masse* – as departments, functions or levels, such as the UK Civil Service's multiple grades – or as individuals in their own right?

Failure to recognize the individuality of people's response to empowerment leads to catch-all approaches that can alienate as many people as they motivate. A useful starting point in designing flexible, individual-centred approaches is to be clear *why* we need to change the behaviour of individuals.

WHY DO WE NEED TO CHANGE THE BEHAVIOUR OF INDIVIDUALS?

Individuals are the basis of the team

The productivity of a team, if it works well, should be greater than the sum of the efforts made by its members. That's why teams are formed – to gain that multiplier effect. There is, however, a danger of focusing on the effectiveness of team-work while neglecting the basic unit that makes a good team – the individual operator. Poorly trained and unmotivated individuals cannot be pulled together into highly efficient and productive teams, no matter how much team-building training they are put through.

It's often individuals who have most direct contact with the customer

In most service encounters, from a professional–client relationship to over-the-counter service at a fast food restaurant, the customers' experience of a company is only as good as the individual who serves them. This alone should make service companies stand up and take notice – and they have done. As we detail in the next chapter, an increasing proportion of service companies are allowing individuals at the front line to take responsibility for the customer encounter on their own. A number of leading hotel chains have given near complete authority to the person on the spot to resolve problems, without bringing in a supervisor. Avis, Lufthansa and BA have experimented with empowering their ground staff to make on-the-spot decisions about compensating disgruntled customers with gifts and cash.

Organizational learning is the sum of the learning of all the individuals within the organization

Our definition of a learning organization is one which helps individuals develop an appetite for beneficial change. Empowerment is a tool that can help bring about a learning organization, but only through the learning of individuals – after all, organizations can't learn, only individuals can.

Lasting change normally occurs with the consent of a majority of the individuals involved

Teams and whole organizations may change, but only individuals can give their consent and commitment to change.

Changing individual behaviours can have a radical, beneficial effect on business performance

Maintains consultant Peter Bennett:

> These days, a standard knee jerk response to recession is rationalization. But in the stampede to cut costs and overheads it is easy to overlook the converse approach – that of improving performance at operator level.
>
> Development of operators and front line staff is an area sadly neglected in most organizations, yet there are huge returns to be made from it. For example, at one company that developed its operators, sales soared by 8 per cent in a year to reach the highest ever share of a highly competitive market. At another site, output increased by 20 per cent, compliments from customers shot up, the previously high employee turnover slumped, costs were cut – and this was all achieved despite a 40 per cent reduction in managerial staff. Yet another firm recorded an almost immediate 6 per cent increase in throughput in a department where operators had undergone a development programme.

As Steven Brandt, a senior lecturer at the Stanford Business School, puts it:

> It is employees' attitudes, rather than say, cash flow or process technology, that make a fundamental, competitive difference between companies. If we want our enterprises to be winners, the evidence is piling up that each of us had better make 'our' company 'my' company to the cadre of souls who constitute the core of our enterprise. The new order of business depends more than ever on assets that wear shoes, on assets that go home at night.[1]

For all these reasons, it makes sense to achieve the involvement of the maximum proportion of employees at all levels. But achieving high levels of individual involvement is far from easy. As Alistair Wright, human resource director at Digital Equipment quips: 'I used to think you could just sprinkle golden dust on employees' heads and say: "Now you're empowered. Go away and multiply." It doesn't work because they don't do it.'[2]

WHY DON'T PEOPLE EMBRACE EMPOWERMENT AUTO-MATICALLY?

Why don't people automatically become involved? The simple answer is that, despite the obvious benefits of empowering front-line staff, the concept still faces resistance from many quarters – from managers, from existing systems and long-standing cultural attitudes, and, all too often, from the shopfloor employees themselves.

This last area of resistance is the most difficult to overcome, for four reasons:

❑ people are wary of change

❑ many employees have reason to be sceptical of empowerment

❑ operators are free to choose whether to be empowered or not

❑ not everybody wants to be empowered.

Recognizing and overcoming these obstacles is an essential first step in tapping the talents of the shop floor.

People are wary of change

Most empowerment initiatives come as part and parcel of a major, often painful, change programme, such as organizational restructuring, redundancies, job redefinitions and the like. Thus the first step in making an empowerment initiative take hold at an individual level is to gain employee commitment to the idea of change in general.

The authors, in an earlier study, found that individuals become supportive of and committed to change, even if it is not entirely in their best interests, when the following criteria are fulfilled:

❏ they understand what the change involves and why it is important

❏ they understand and accept the implications for themselves and for their colleagues

❏ they believe they will be supported in implementing the change

❏ they recognize top management's commitment to making the change work

❏ they feel they have some direct influence on how the change is carried out where it affects them

Many employees have reason to be sceptical of empowerment

For many organizations, gaining acceptance of change is complicated by employees' unhappy experiences with false starts in the past. Empowerment has earned a bad name on many factory floors, on many occasions having been used when companies wanted to hand over responsibility for tasks without authority or ownership. It is scarcely surprising, then, that employees sometimes see it in terms of delegated liabilities rather than as a form of job enrichment – or, more bluntly, as a means to off-load responsibility without reward to front-line staff. As one factory employee observed: 'Empowerment is fine for managers and supervisors because it allows them to delegate work downwards. But when it gets to our level, there's no one left to delegate it to.'

In an empowerment experiment in a major UK retail chain, one of the most promising youngsters in the store handed in her notice with the comment: 'I liked my job at first, because I didn't want to have extra responsibilities. Now the work team is doing a lot of the manager's job, and I don't feel comfortable any more.'

In common with many others, this company went through

a period of initial enthusiasm and high motivation by some work groups, followed later by demands for more pay to compensate them for 'doing the manager's job.' The employees' concerns were justified. After all, the company had made no secret of the fact that it was empowering people in order to increase sales and productivity. If its focus was on the hard benefits, why should the focus of the employees not be the same?

Operators are free to choose whether to be empowered or not

Empowerment is perhaps one of the trickiest operational changes to make by virtue of the fact that it is personal, and entirely optional.

Empowered or not, people at the lower levels of an organization already have tremendous power, but organizational cultures and structures limit the extent to which they are willing to use this power. Empowerment is about releasing, not giving power, says Coverdale's Richard Carver.

Cary Cherniss, chair of the organizational behaviour programme in the Graduate School of Applied Professional Psychology at Rutgers University, agrees:

> People choose for themselves whether to be empowered or not. Management can remove stifling regulations, policies and procedures. Managers can ask employees what they think, listen to the answers and act on good suggestions, but beyond that sort of thing, attempts to empower people from above are destined to fail. It's very difficult for either management or an outside consultant to empower employees. It's sort of a contradiction. You can't give power to someone else. If you're giving them the power, it implies that you have the power and they don't and if you can give it, you can take it away.[3]

According to John Burdett, vice-president of the Canadian packaging conglomerate, the Lawson Mardon Group:

> As individuals, and more often as a team, operators have the power to work enthusiastically or not, to take an interest in the company or not, to watch out for quality or not. It is not that employees do not have power, but that all too often the power they have is channelled in such a way that the aims and

goals of the organization and those of employees are in conflict.[4]

Bringing those two sets of goals into line is the essence of
most successful empowerment programmes.

Not everyone wants to be empowered

Even if employees can be made to see that empowerment is
in their best interests, there will invariably remain some individuals who feel it is not for them. (It is significant that only
49 per cent of employees surveyed in the Employment in
Britain survey wanted more say in decisions affecting their
work.) They may feel they are not being paid enough to take
on extra responsibility, they may prefer to put their intellectual energies into activities outside work, or as Cherniss
points out, they may simply be frightened by the prospect of
increased, unfamiliar, power and responsibility.

'If employees lack the knowledge and skills to perform
effectively in situations where they have a lot of autonomy,
then giving them more autonomy and control can really
backfire,' he says. 'So what we need to do is to give workers
a sense of efficacy, to make them feel that they have the
knowledge and the skills to control things in the organization
and to use whatever autonomy they have to perform at high
levels.'

WHAT MAKES PEOPLE CHANGE BEHAVIOUR?

There are a number of discrete steps that most people must
follow before changing behaviour:

❑ **Awareness of the need for change**, at both an organizational and a personal level. Individuals can only make
genuine, long-term changes if they understand the
underlying purpose and reason.

❑ **Acceptance of the need for change**, at both levels. An
individual might understand the need for change at an
intellectual level, but won't actually make the behaviour-
ial change until he or she can come to accept the need for

it at an emotional level. Real change comes from internalizing the problem and accepting responsibility for doing something about it.

❏ **Commitment to change:** knowing what you ought to do is not the same as making up your mind to do it. 'Real change happens in the heart, not in the brain,' says consultant Wally Cork. 'When people come to an intellectual understanding about the need for change, they may indeed change; but effective, long-term change will only happen when they really believe in their hearts that they need to change their behaviour.'

❏ **Learning and planning:** it is necessary to break down the process of learning – both the absorption of knowledge and skills and the opportunity to practise them – into manageable stages.

Consultant Milo Lynch uses a three part learning model to help people take on new information and behaviours. For each task, he advises his clients to set:

1. purposes – *why* they are doing the task

2. end results – what they hope to end up with

3. success criteria – to measure how successful they have been.

❏ **Feedback:** it is too easy to convince yourself you've changed. Individuals need objective data, from managers, peers and subordinates, to tell them if they really have changed, and how much.

Most importantly, however, it is commitment to the purpose behind change that leads to lasting behavioural change. Says Carver: 'Individuals change their behaviour when they have a reason to do so and that reason means something to them.' Commitment to change, he says, is based on an awareness and acceptance of the reasons behind the change and of the benefits to be gained from implementing the change.

Consultant Wally Cork has a dramatic way of demonstrating the importance of purpose to training course delegates:

I tell them to jump in the lake. Of course the team look at me like as if I'm quite mad, until I explain why: 'There's a child drowning'. Once everyone in the group is clear about why a task is important, they just dash off and do it. Once people understand purposes, getting things done is easy.

KEYS TO UNLOCKING THE POTENTIAL OF INDIVIDUALS

Overcoming the barriers to empowerment within individuals requires a coherent approach to:

- ❑ ensuring that employees understand and commit to the purpose behind the empowerment initiative
- ❑ building initial skills and confidence
- ❑ gaining commitment to the changes
- ❑ setting the parameters
- ❑ establishing a relevant reward system
- ❑ continuous learning
- ❑ supporting people with information.

Ensuring that employees understand and commit to the purpose behind the empowerment initiative

People will put far more into a task if they understand the purpose behind it, says Carver. He relates the example of a factory that desperately needed to reduce its operating costs:

> The managers decided they had done everything they could, but they could not compete with cheap labour from abroad. They concluded that the only answer was to close the factory and make people redundant.
>
> The work force, however, insisted that they could operate the plant profitably given the chance. And, after extensive discussions and some external assistance, the employees managed to reduce operating costs by 40 per cent. This was done by judicious subcontracting, investment in new, more efficient equipment, and cost cutting. The purpose behind the measures – saving their own jobs – inspired them to do what they might not have thought they were capable of otherwise.

Building skills and confidence

UK dairy company Dairycrest Ingredients is reaping the benefits of empowering its shopfloor operators. One group of operators at the company's Whitland dairy, on their own initiative, devised various ways of reducing the cost of detergent and shaved a massive 25 per cent off an annual £100,000 detergent bill.

> That example was measurable in monetary terms, but attitudes at this creamery have also changed enormously. Every operator is switched on to doing well. They see that their own objectives of being in a job and bringing home money for their families are in line with getting on with colleagues and working together to find the best solution to any problem that might arise,

says Peter Bennett, the consultant on the development project.

> In any effort at empowerment, it is inevitable that you will come across some people with negative attitudes, but in almost every case that is because they do not understand their own potential or how it can be developed.
>
> I have seen operators who would once have rejected almost any management suggestion change their attitudes completely. They have become pro-active in seeking ways of improving their work and increasing productivity – once they became aware that managers were prepared to invest in their development and that there would therefore be opportunities to do better both from the point of view of job satisfaction and the chance of greater reward.

In another session at Dairycrest, Bennett suggested that a team look at an issue which was vaguely connected with their department. One team member exclaimed: 'I'm not f**king doing that – it's not my job.' In that situation, says Bennett, you can either move on and forget it, or confront the issue and iron out the problem. So he retorted. 'Well, I'm not wasting my f**king time with you then.' Shocked, the protestor fell silent for the rest of the session.

As Bennett was leaving later that evening, the man came up to him and apologized for his behaviour, explaining that he was in the middle of a separation from his wife. He then invited the consultant round to his house. Over a drink, the pair discussed empowerment at the creamery, as well as a host of other subjects. Following the incident the employee in question began to thrive in the newly empowered environment. As Bennett explained:

> You have to meet the operator on his level. Often he feels scared or threatened by what is happening. Other times he might believe that his contribution will be scorned. So it is important for the team leader or manager to listen constructively to every suggestion, otherwise the front-line employee will feel his contribution is not worthwhile and may well reject the idea of empowerment.
>
> Of course there will always be people who refuse to take responsibility for their actions and refuse to be empowered – these people will, sadly, either be edged out by their workmates or just leave because the new regime doesn't suit them.
>
> Fortunately, it is a very small minority who really don't want to be empowered – most people welcome the chance to have a say in what happens in their job. In fact, many are flattered to be told by management that their skills are respected and to be asked to start playing a greater role. And empowerment is not necessarily linked to higher wages either, as people basically enjoy bringing their mind to bear on a task.

However, a few unfortunate management teams have found that a substantial turnover of staff is the only way to make empowerment work, as Dave Wiegand of Advanced Network Design Inc. (ADNET) discovered.[5] In 1988, Wiegand figured he had maybe 90 days before he had to shut down. The La Mirada, California telecommunications company was withering, thanks largely to his 'demand management' style. The more he pushed, the less productive his then 35 employees became. Unsure of how to halt the company's slide, he hired a turnaround expert.

In designing a strategy for ADNET, the consultant invoked the concept of job autonomy. If Wiegand could match the right individuals to the right positions, then give them authority and responsibility, he was told, the likely result would be stronger motivation, better work quality, higher job satisfaction, and lower turnover.

Wiegand, a self-confessed control freak, bought into the idea – reluctantly. Yet the eventual shift was so drastic that a large number of employees couldn't adapt and ended up leaving. But in the process, Wiegand learned a few things about human behaviour. First, implementers, unlike initiators, can't easily handle the freedom. Second, before hiring for any job, it's critical to pinpoint the specific traits that the position requires. 'We identify 15 or 20 traits,' Wiegand says. 'Does it require someone who's detail oriented or who has good time-management skills? If so, we build an interview that probes for those, and we put candidates through tests designed to assess whether they have those traits.' ADNET perked up as Wiegand phased in the strategy and restaffed with new people.

Gaining commitment to change

Stanford Business School's Steven Brandt has found a common denominator in empowerment programmes that have succeeded in gaining shopfloor-level commitment:[6]

> Xerox's benchmarking, Ford's chimney breaking and virtually every other successful employee involvement programme I have studied, have all tapped employee commitment to change by giving every employee at least two 'jobs' – two areas of responsibility, and the support each person needs to do both jobs well.
>
> In every case the second level is a broader, more total, enterprise-oriented challenge. And the broad success of such a wide variety of techniques and programs suggests that people do, as I have long believed, rise to meet expectations.

John Burdett of the Lawson Mardon Group agrees:

> In an empowered environment, there are two critical components in any job. The first is the core activities, which are those that must be performed successfully if the employee is to achieve the basic purpose of the job. The second is an area of flexibility based on the employee's competency which can be expanded into. This is an area of the job where initiative is not only possible, but within an empowered environment, actively encouraged. Job overlap, rather than being avoided at all costs, becomes an opportunity for information sharing, synergy and innovation.[7]

A look at some successful initiatives bears this out:

❑ At Johnsonville Foods, a sausage maker in Wisconsin, volunteers from the shop floor write the manufacturing budget. At first a financial manager walked them through the process, but now he just observes.

❑ At Walkers Smiths Snack Foods, the people charged with a major product improvement project were the operators who made the product every day. When they weren't analysing waste points or making presentations to the board, they were mixing, frying and packaging the goods.

❑ Granite Rock, a California producer of construction and paving materials, delivers such matchless quality and service it can charge a premium of up to 6 per cent on commodities like concrete and asphalt, and has gained market share every year since 1987. In 1992 it won the Malcolm Baldrige National Quality Award.

  How? In an industry rarely associated with brainpower throughout the ranks, Granite Rock has turned itself into a think tank at all levels. The company employs 397 people and all actively participate in at least one of its more than 100 quality teams. Its managers believe the only way to compete in a cut-throat industry is to encourage all employees to keep learning and injecting their know-how back into the business.[8]

Setting the parameters

What impressed Bob Freese, CEO of Alphatronix Inc, in North Carolina, is how hard people will work when they're allowed to set their own objectives. 'We let employees tell us when they can accomplish a project and what resources they need. Virtually always, they set higher goals than we would ever set for them.'[9]

But how much should employees be left to set their own goals? 'You can't just hire the best people and let them have a go at it,' says Curt Rawley, CEO Of Avid Technology, in Massachusetts 'What's called for is a set of checks and balances.'[10]

Paul Taffinder, a senior consultant with Coopers Lybrand, agrees that parameters and boundaries are an essential part of empowerment. 'When people are given the conditions in which they are able to do the job to a very high standard, they are much clearer about their linkages to their suppliers and their customers. You can empower and say, those are the parameters you have to play with. It's up to you how you actually optimize that. That's a much more defined situation. Providing empowerment in an over-complex situation where you are not providing some ground rules and guidance to people is really a recipe for disaster.'[11]

That's why, he says, de-skilling and empowerment are not necessarily at cross-purposes:

> To some extent de-skilling goes with empowerment because the job scope is being better defined. For example, it can be argued that scanners have empowered supermarket checkout clerks. The job is technically less skilled – running purchases over a reader rather than touch typing prices – but frees up the clerk to give more attention to customers, and to deal with, for example, more complex payment methods.

Nor are narrowly defined job descriptions necessarily incompatible with empowerment, says Carver:

> It is a question of how much of the job is open for innovative thought. In industries such as the petrochemical industry there may be certain procedures of a bureaucratic or statutory nature that need to be implemented to comply with the law. However, there will be other parts of the job (how we can improve safety performance, for example) where empowerment may have a real role to play. The difficulty in such organizations is how to get the appropriate balance between people's willingness to innovate and take personal responsibility for beneficial change in part of the job while knowing that they are screwed to the floor with detailed procedures in another part of it.

Thus job descriptions play an essential role in empowerment. Some would argue they are even more important in an empowered, than in an unempowered workplace. Empowered job descriptions, however, come with an essential difference: They are written as a set of objectives and expectations, rather than as a rigid set of rules. They detail more what the employee is expected to accomplish, than how he or she is expected to accomplish it. They describe employees' roles, rights and responsibilities, as well as tasks.

Empowered job descriptions should include each of the following elements:

❑ **The purpose of the job**: what is the person who fulfils it expected to add to the overall purpose of the organization? How is he or she expected to help fulfil the organization's aims?

❑ **A description of role**: that is, what is expected of this employee? For example, a role statement for a service engineer might read:

— You will assist the company in its customer promise of responding to all customer call-outs within three hours.
— You will enhance the customer's perception of the company by providing efficient, professional and friendly service.
— You will regard each customer encounter as an opportunity to increase the value of our service.

❑ **A description of responsibility**: that is, what the employee owes in terms of support to other people in the organization. Again, taking the example of a service engineer:

— You will provide timely, accurate feedback to the technical and marketing departments whenever you encounter opportunities for improvement in products or services.

❑ **A description of rights**: that is, what the employee is entitled to demand of other individuals and departments in the company.
The service engineer might have a right to:

— Accurate, immediate information on spares availability
— Detailed information on the customer location and any previous service visits made

— Support from his/her manager for decisions made in the field to recover the goodwill of a dissatisfied customer.

Norman Metzger, a healthcare management expert, advises on a more structured and controlled way to give employees a clear idea of what is expected of them while giving them additional responsibility.[12]

1. Set a clear and simple objective.

2. Don't automatically choose your best worker for the task, as a challenging task may give an average person a chance to shine. Ask for volunteers and you may be surprised by who raises their hand.

3. Assign the task and explain to the person why you've chosen him or her. This will tell the person that you value his or her judgement and aren't just pushing work his or her way.

4. If necessary, train the worker to prepare him or her for the task. Additional responsibility should build confidence, so select an assignment that will stretch, but not break, the employee. When discussing the project, ask the employee for ideas. He or she may see the problem in an entirely different light. This also ensures that he or she understands the project.

5. Provide needed guidance. This doesn't mean telling the person how to do it. It means giving him or her all the facts he or she needs, suggesting, carefully, possible approaches, and describing the expected results.

6. Establish how much freedom the employee will have with company resources, how often you'll follow up, and how performance will be measured.

7. Establish controls, such as budget, deadline, and when and how a formal review will take place.

8. Set up a file to remind yourself to check up on the progress of the project.

9. Provide feedback, whether positive or negative.

10. Evaluate the finished project. Notes made in your file will remind you of what went right and what went wrong with the project.

Establish a relevant reward system

Job descriptions, roles, responsibilities and expectations – all beg the question: what's in it for the individual?

Greater involvement in the workplace, a chance to own a project, to use one's creativity and be recognized for one's ideas are all valued by most workers and each can, in the long term, motivate employees to give their all to a job. This, however, takes time, and many companies find they need something more immediately tangible to gain initial acceptance for the greater expectations empowerment makes of employees.

As *Inc* magazine's Tom Ehrenfeld notes: 'Nothing so nakedly displays what a company stands for in terms of hierarchy and fairness as its pay system, and nothing demoralized employees faster than compensation schemes that fail to be fair.'[13]

Compensation schemes range from nominal rewards for individual efforts and ideas, to gain-sharing and profit-related pay, to out and out employee ownership. The most effective schemes provide large enough sums to be meaningful, are seen to be fair, and are tied to work in such a way that employees can see the connections between their own efforts, company profits, and their personal pay packets.

For example, employees at Mars UK receive a pay rise every time the company hits a predetermined band of growth. Former Mars corporate affairs manager Locksley Ryan explains:

> The principle behind the pay structure is that you gear the business to deliver a certain level of growth and everybody is aware of that at all stages. In an ideal situation, you not only see how the business is doing, but you are able to relate it to you own activity.[14]

Robert Frey, owner of Cine-Made Corporation in Cincinnati, Ohio, looked long and hard for a profit-sharing plan that would meet his needs. He wanted, he says, 'to give employees a reason to care.'[15]

> I wanted to share this company with my employees. In the beginning, it was the pain I wanted to share as much as the profit. I wanted the workers to worry. Did anyone of them ever spend a moment on a weekend wondering how the company was doing, asking herself if she'd made the right decisions the week before? Maybe I was unrealistic, but I wanted that level of involvement.

Frey says he didn't like the looks of other corporate profit-sharing plans he investigated:

> All the plans I read about sounded manipulative. The rules were subject to change without notice. The profits shared were whatever management declared them to be. The plans were handouts, a form of charity. Not surprisingly, they completely failed to convey any sense of the cause and effect relationship between productivity and profits, between work and success. Another problem was the complexity of the rules. Worst of all, the plans never paid out much money. And my idea was to pay out lots of money, enough to create a tangible connection between the way people worked and the profits they shared. Enough to get everyone passionately involved in the effort to cut costs, increase sales and make money.
>
>   I wanted to do something radical. I wanted to make profit sharing – the variable component – so big (and growing) that it would serve as an incentive to keep wages – the fixed component – frozen. This would lower the risk of doing business, while at the same time offering bigger and bigger rewards to our employees. My employees would share my profits, but they would also share my anxieties.

Frey opted to share 30 per cent of his profits with employees – the most he could possibly spare after taxes, investment and his own salary:

> I wanted to establish a pattern of cause and effect by establishing a pattern of big wage increases, bigger than anything they'd ever seen, but only after the money had been earned. Profit-sharing was only partly a matter of fairness. For me, an even more critical goal was to open my employees' eyes to

where wages came from and to the trade-offs they would have to make between benefits and profits.

Perhaps the most encouraging result of profit-sharing plans is that, in company after company, once the schemes have met their objectives of 'giving employees a reason to care', the cash itself becomes secondary. In 1992, at Ericsson General Electric, the recession meant that employees hadn't seen a gain-sharing bonus in two years.[16] Yet that didn't seem to affect the workforce's enthusiasm for the company's profit-sharing plan. Although employees told *Training* magazine's Bob Filipczak that they missed the bonus and hoped to earn it again, it didn't appear to be foremost in their minds. Even without a financial pay-off, they still submitted 4,900 ideas that year – the highest number since the system's inception.

Of course the mere promise of payouts doesn't ensure incremental improvement by workers, unless those workers have some guidelines for helping to cut costs and some training to help them do it.

Continuous learning

It is both ineffective and unfair to expect more input from employees without giving them the skills and techniques they need to do what's expected of them. Fortunately, companies are investing more in training and developing their employees. And, though this is not always done with the intention of empowering them, that is often the end result.

Training does more than just pass on skills – it also demonstrates the company's commitment to, and trust in, its employees, writes *Inc* magazine's Tom Ehrenfeld:

Training lays bare the basic compact between a company and its employees, exposing the company's commitment to the future and revealing trust that workers can learn new skills, take on more responsibility – and risk failure. There's risk on the employer's side, too. Plenty of CEOs can gripe about employees who took a walk once they completed their training.'[17]

Employees too gripe that their training is often patchy or *ad hoc*. Many find they get more out of training courses if they are aware of the context and purpose of the training. As one group of factory workers told the authors: 'They send us on courses, but they don't tell us what the end goal is supposed to be. We would get a lot more out of it if we knew what we were aiming for.'

According to the Employment in Britain Survey, many more employees are now receiving training from their employers, and for longer periods than they did in the mid-1980s. However, there remains a substantial training gap. One in five of those who want training in the future feel that they are unlikely to get it. Also, those without qualifications or in jobs at lower skill levels have much the lowest chances of receiving training.[18]

For empowerment to work, companies don't necessarily need massive formal training, says Marc Tucker, president of the National Center on Education and the Economy in Rochester, New York. 'There must only be opportunities for people to learn.'[19]

Johnsonville Foods follows this principle, offering employees opportunities to learn for the sake of learning, in the belief that a lifelong learning habit will reflect well in their jobs. Johnsonville's personnel department has become the 'Personal Development Lifelong Learning Department'.

> Workers see a counsellor who helps them to articulate their goals and dreams – be those becoming a senior vice-president, putting their kids through college or learning to grow roses. Each employee receives a small allowance – $100 a year – to spend on a personal growth project. Some of them enter college or graduate school; others join a cooking class. For big expenses, like education, employees may also get scholarships.[20]

What does Johnsonville get in return? A lot, reports chief executive Ralph Stayer. 'Our people are an appreciating asset, not a depreciating one. They're more willing to change, to question. When they see that they can change something in their personal lives, they bring that attitude to work.'

Rover UK has taken up the same principle, offering employees an annual allowance to study whatever they choose, and management at Luitink Manufacturing Company in Wisconsin takes an equally holistic view of training.[21] Management at Luitink redefined training as the learning that goes on between employees when they work together productively. 'Usually the first thing that comes to mind is a lot of technical training,' says Luitink vice president of manufacturing Joe Hauk. 'But as we changed from an autocratic company to one with a lot of empowerment and team building, we began looking at training as understanding how employees interact with each other.' Consequently, Luitink now thinks of training as ensuring that knowledge flows from worker to worker. 'It appears to work,' reports Ehrenfeld:

> Five years ago, press operator John Hausner did no more than his defined duties, backing off during machine changeovers to let the die makers ply their trade. But now he's absorbing some of the skills – and responsibilities, of his teammates as he learns how to change the dies himself, freeing the die makers to focus on more skill-intensive tasks like sharpening dies.

Says Hauk: 'Once we believed in hiring people for the skills they had. We now believe we can take someone with the attitude and the desire to learn and make that person into the best machine operator there is.'

For a snapshot of the potential benefits, look at the profit improvements one IBM plant gained from a new attitude to training.

In 1985, IBM's printed circuit board plant in Austin Texas, was overstaffed, under-productive and losing $60 million a year.[22] With three indirect workers for every line employee, it was clear that the company needed fewer, more skilled, employees. Instead of replacing its workers, which was very much against corporate policy, or moving to a lower wage area, such as Mexico, the company opted to launch a re-education programme designed to combine a cut in the indirect workforce with retraining for the others so they could take on broader tasks.

The programme, called Manufacturing Technical Associates, or MTA, cut 200 job classifications down to seven grades. Those on the lowest grade spend more than 90 per cent of their time on production work, and the remainder on technical tasks such as materials analysis. As the worker acquires more skills, and higher pay, the proportions gradually alter. But even those in the first grade require up to 40 hours of skill-based classroom training, as well as classes in basic maths and reading.

Abe Clay, the plant's manufacturing manager, says any deficiency in basic education was less striking than the untapped potential of the 800-strong direct workforce. 'There were a lot of people who you would have said were incapable of doing this or that until you tested it. It made me think that we have not really tapped the resident skills of a lot of the workforce.'

And the new structure has clarified what was previously a murky grading system and made explicit what the company expects of workers. 'It tells me my limitations,' says Grade Five worker Jerry Schiappa. 'It is the first time I have known what I need to do to get to the next level,' he says.

The programme exceeded all expectations. In seven years, productivity has doubled, stockpiles have been reduced by 40 per cent, production has increased and there has been a 5 per cent quality improvement. IBM has now put about two thirds of its 30,000 direct workers through MTA or similar programmes.

Triton Industries in Chicago has had similar successes.[23] When Chico Lopez started work at Triton nine years ago, the only material he could cut was hair. Five years as a barber had given him none of the skills needed for the cutting and shaping of metal. Three months after he landed work at Triton as a temporary labourer, though, Lopez started as a full-time machine operator, and from there his professional education began. First came a class in tool set-up safety through a local trade association, then courses in precision instrument and blueprint reading at Triton. Finally, Lopez studied management courses in everything from motivating employees to total quality management (TQM). Today, as the lead man in the stamping department, he earns about three times his starting wage. Lopez's rise to a well-paying, skill-intensive job is far from unique. Virtually all of Triton's supervisors earned their positions by learning new skills, from, or with the support of, the company. The reason is simple: 'We could not stay the way we were even two years ago,' says production manager Jeri Barr.

At Triton, workers who complete the first eight weeks of a 32-week in-house sheet metal craftsmanship course receive $225; as they take more courses, the incentives increase.

Ashton Photo in Salem Oregon also rewards employees for learning, basing pay not just on the skills workers use, but also on those they learn and teach.[24] Employees define and rank the skills vital to the company's manufacturing process. To determine pay, they grade themselves on how proficient they consider themselves in those skills. Because the company seeks continual improvement through cross-training, the highest rating values mastery of a skill as the ability to teach it.

> 'People know that if they learn more, they can make more,' says Karen Welch, who was promoted from photo assembler to line leader in one year. 'In that year I learned editing, data entry and printing – something from each area and how to bring it all together.' Ashton owner Steve Ashton says the plan has had a real pay-off: In the past six years the company has doubled sales without taking on any new employees.

Even the most thorough training programme will not, however, create an empowered organization on its own, writes management journalist Peter Kizilos:

> Education certainly has some power to change behaviour, but altering people's orientation toward empowerment – turning a bureaucratic goldbricker into a risk-seeking, initiative-taking, problem-solving, go-getter – is no simple training task. That would be true even if there were no obstacles outside the trainer's control – and there are plenty.
>
> Organizational inertia tends to discourage people from acting in an empowered fashion. Individual fiefdoms carefully nurtured over time don't suddenly crumble overnight, and the attitudes of control-oriented managers may be nearly impossible to change.[25]

Supporting people with information

Many empowerment initiatives fall flat, despite extensive training because organizations fail to give employees access to the information they need to make use of their new-found skills.

For many empowering companies, on the other hand, opening the books to employees is a first step in heralding change. At Ford of Britain, for example, one of the company's first turnaround moves was to adopt a policy of disclosing all business information to its workforce. As Andy Richards, plant convenor of the Transport and General Workers Union at Bridgend, says: 'As far as the management union team is concerned, in this plant we share one objective, and that is that the plant must prosper.'[26]

Hal Rosenbluth, president of Rosenbluth Travel in Philadelphia, has an unusual method of sharing information with front-line staff.

> He believes in an open door policy, but with 2,500 employees spread over 300 cities, he estimates it would take a year and half to see everybody. So three days a week he invites one or two associates to visit him. These 'Associates of the Day' sit in on client calls, meetings or whatever is on his agenda that day. They're asked to honour the confidentiality of the proceedings, but get to observe virtually all of Rosenbluth's business – including, in one case, the performance review of a vice president who did not object.
>
> Associates also have access to profit and loss statements and are given a chance between meetings to ask questions or make comments about what they've seen. The program, says Rosenbluth, 'helps them understand what goes into the decision-making process,' while giving him 'instant input' from the front line. Plus, he says, 'talking to someone throughout the day and getting their insights gives me a good idea of who the future leaders of this company will be.'[27]

At Buckingham Foods, management realized that its ability to make profit targets lay in upgrading productivity but, says managing director Peter Halman: 'The lack of relevant and up to date data was preventing supervisors from making vital production decisions. We recognized that to get the most out of the business we had to have accurate performance-based data, which would allow employees to make the right decisions at the right time.'[28]

Buckingham's line staff were given the latest ordering and scheduling figures and then got on with organizing production around them, bringing in the right number of staff and ordering enough ingredients to meet orders without wastage. As a result, the company, which makes sandwiches for sale through high street outlets, managed to squeeze £800,000 in savings out of a £30 million turnover in 30 weeks, without major spending on technology or capital equipment. The company also recorded a 25 per cent improvement in its annual profit target and was able to take on more business while maintaining its existing staffing level of about 500.

'It was very much about getting people on the shop floor to make decisions and manage the process,' says Halman. 'They understood it best and they were the ones who could make it more effective.'

CONCLUSION

Individuals form the basis of any empowerment initiative. And, though it is individuals who generate some of the fiercest resistance to empowerment, they are also the ones who stand to gain the most from it. The key to transforming resistance into positive change is a clear understanding of the purpose behind the empowerment initiative.

This chapter has dealt primarily with issues facing production or back room employees. In the next chapter, we will look at the special needs of service employees, and the organizations that employ them.

References

1. Brandt, S.C., 'Bring your brains to work please', *Stanford Business School Magazine,* December 1991.

2. Author unkown, 'Empowerment, a leap of faith?', *Management Training*, August 1993.

3. Kizilos, P., 'Crazy about empowermeet', *Training*, December 1990.

4. Burdett, J.O., 'What is empowerment anyway?', *Journal of European Industrial-Training,* Vol 15, no 6, 1991.

5. Finegan, J.O., 'People power', *Inc,* July 1993.

6. Brandt, S.C., 'Bring your brains to work please', op. cit.

7. Burdett, J.O., op. cit.

8. Austin, N.K., 'Where employee training works', *Working Woman,* May 1993.

9. Fenn, D., 'Bottoms up', *Inc,* July 1993.

10. Ibid.

11. Oates, D., *Leadership: The Art of Delegation,* Century Business Books, London, 1993.

12. Metzger, N., 'Hanging on to what you've got', *Health and Manpower Management,* January 1990

13. Ehrenfeld, T., 'Cashing in', *Inc,* July 1993.

14. Jackson, S., 'Empowerment to the people?', *Director,* April 1991.

15. Frey, R., 'Empowerment or else', *Harvard Business Review,* September-October 1993.

16. Filipczak, R., 'Ericsson General Electric, the evolution of empowerment', *Training,* September 1993.

17. Ehrenfeld, T., 'School's in', *Inc,* July 1993.

18. *Employee Commitment and the Skills Revolution,* the Policy Studies Institute, June 1993 (part of the Employment in Britain Survey).

19. Ehrenfeld, T., 'Cashing in', op. cit.

20. Stewart, T.A., 'A user's guide to power', *Fortune,* 6 November 1989.

21. Ehrenfeld, Tom., 'School's in', op. cit.

22. Gapper, J. 'Workers who want to make the grade', *Financial Times,* 5 October 1992.

23. Ehrenfeld, T., 'School's in', op. cit.

24. Ehrenfeld, T., 'Cashing in', op. cit.

25. Kizilos, P., 'Crazy about empowerment', op. cit.

26. 'Bridgend spears Ford revolution', *The Times*, 24 September 1992.

27. Peters, T., 'Associates spend a day in the executive suite', *On Achieving Excellence,* August 1990.

28. Hewson, D., 'Try a taste of something different', *The Sunday Times*, 17 October 1993.

7
EMPOWERMENT IN THE SERVICE SECTOR

To free someone from rigorous control ... and to give that person freedom to take responsibility for his ideas, decisions, and actions, is to release hidden resources that would otherwise remain inaccessible to both the individual and the organization.

Jan Carlzon, former CEO of SAS Scandinavian Airlines System

It is impossible to get people's best efforts, involvement, and caring concern for things you believe important to your customers and the long-term interests of your organization when you write policies and procedures that treat them like thieves and bandits.

Tom Peters, management consultant and author

We finally figured out that for every pair of hands we hire, we get a brain for free. So why not use it?

Anonymous CEO

In some ways service companies have more to gain from empowerment that manufacturing organizations. For most, the only way to create a competitive edge is through their people and the quality of service they can provide. Many leading service organizations, including the Holiday Inn, Marriot Hotels and Avis Rent-a-Car, have created the edge they need by allowing their staff to decide, on the spot, what is best for the customers.

Yet empowerment in the service industry is a risky business. If, for example, an empowered sheet metal worker wants to try a new procedure, he can do it in a controlled environment, at the cost of some time and raw materials. Service workers, however, must experiment in real time, in front of real customers. If they get it wrong, there is no safety net.

As Richard Segalowitch of Club Med told a 1993 conference audience: 'In an industrial business, when the CEO defines its product, it is likely that the result will be in conformity. In the service industry, it is unlikely to obtain the same result. Also, because services are performed in the customer's presence, errors are inevitable.'

Empowerment in service organizations has certainly generated more publicity than that on the factory floor. It does, after all, make delightful advertising copy – witness the Avis staffer who flew a lost teddy bear home to its owner, or the Marriot bell boy who lent a guest his own cuff-links. Dry statistics, however, indicate that the risks of empowerment still outweigh the benefits in the eyes of most service providers, and the service industry as a whole has been relatively slow to take it up.

According to American business academics David Bowen and Edward Lawler, a 1989 survey of companies in the *Fortune* 1000 revealed that 'service firms are lagging in the use of employee involvement practices; and manufacturing firms use quality circles, participation groups, and self-managing work teams far more than service firms.'[1]

This, they say, is because the manufacturing sector faces more intense global competition than the service sector, putting greater pressure on it to find new ways of doing things. It is also easier to see the pay-offs from empowerment in manufacturing than in service – productivity is simpler to measure than customer perceptions.

The trend looks set to change, however. According to Bowen and Lawler, service firms are now facing more and fiercer competition, and the results of empowerment are now easier to measure as service companies have become more sophisticated in tracking the benefits of service quality. Arriving late has its advantages, they add: 'As service businesses consider empowerment, they can look at high involvement manufacturing organizations as labs in which the various empowerment approaches have been tested and developed.'

Not all the lessons learned on the factory floor will apply, however, as there are a number of empowerment issues – both costs and benefits – that relate only to service organizations.

One of the biggest worries with empowering customer-facing staff is the risk, or at least the fear by management, that staff will be more accommodating than necessary, to make life easier for themselves – that they will, in short, give away the shop. That is why providing front-line staff with guidelines, and clearly defined limits within which they can use their discretion, is essential in empowering front-line service staff.

Empowerment in service organizations can mean anything from allowing a £20 ceiling to compensate an unhappy customer, to giving staff free reign to do whatever they feel is appropriate. Most organizations fall somewhere between the two, choosing a set of guidelines that best strike a balance between the needs of customers, staff and the company.

Robert A. Brymer, a faculty member in the Department of Hospitality Administration at Florida State University, describes two alternative empowerment structures that can be applied to help empowered staff make decisions and help management maintain a degree of consistency and control: structured empowerment and flexible empowerment.[2]

Structured empowerment

This provides specific guidelines for front-line employees. It gives them the ability to make decisions, but within specified and detailed limits. Guidelines tell staff exactly what they can do to resolve each of the most commonly experienced customer problems. The guidelines tell them when to make complete adjustments without a quibble, when to refer to a supervisor, and when, and by how much, to make a monetary adjustment. At the Hilton Hotel at Walt Disney World Village, for example, the guidelines include:

❑ A guest announces during check-out that he or she experienced a room-related problem – offer an upgrade for the next visit, or adjust current bill by a maximum of $100.

❑ A guest complains about something unrelated to the room – adjust the bill by up to $50.

❑ A guest claims he incurred no mini-bar charges – make the adjustment.

❑ A guest complains about a rude or insensitive employee – refer problem to assistant manager.

Guidelines like these enable staff to solve problems on the spot and give customers the satisfaction of having their problems dealt with promptly, but they also help managers to retain control on both procedures and purse strings.

One hotel chain, however, found that by giving reception staff a strict monetary limit within which they could use their own discretion in satisfying customer complaints often resulted in escalation of the problem, first to a supervisor, then to a duty manager. In all cases, the duty manager settled the matter in the customer's favour. But by the time the manager intervened, the customers were already sufficiently irritated and embarrassed that more than 50 per cent said they would probably not use the hotel again.

Flexible empowerment

Flexible empowerment, on the other hand, allows employees more latitude in making decisions that directly affect customer service. In an organization using flexible empowerment, management issues very broad guidelines and limits, and employees are expected, and trained to, use good business sense in choosing the best course of action in satisfying a guest. Brymer explains:

> In flexible empowerment, the employee should ask the customer: 'What may I do for you to resolve the problem?' and is authorized to take the necessary steps to satisfy the customer. Employees are expected to consult supervisors only in the most extreme circumstances (for example, if a guest insists that his entire $500 bill should be waived because the hotel's pillows are uncomfortable). Otherwise, employees have the authority to make reasonable decisions to satisfy guests. Managers may choose to impose a top limit on the monetary value of the adjustment that an employee may make.
>
> With flexible empowerment, the autonomy and power given to empowered employees go far beyond the authority to make

adjustments of cash register transactions. Rather, the idea is to encourage employees to improve customer service in as many different ways as possible.

There are, however, risks that staff will go too far in trying to please customers. One hotel chain examined how restaurant staff dealt with customer complaints about the food and drink. It found that staff who went overboard in compensating unhappy customers did as much damage as those who under-compensated. Many of the over-compensated customers said they were embarrassed about coming back. An obvious solution was to be prescriptive about the level of compensation to give in specific circumstances. The hotel group, however, concluded that the real key was to train staff to pitch compensation correctly, and better use their discretionary power to react to individual circumstances.

With either structured or flexible empowerment, three additional factors must be in place if empowerment is to work in a service organization: managers must ensure staff have the information they need, they must ensure someone owns each customer service problem that arises, and they must allow employees the freedom to make mistakes.

Bowen and Lawler describe the bottom-line gains possible from empowering service employees:

Quicker responses to customer needs during service delivery

'Spontaneous, creative, rule-breaking can turn a potentially frustrated or angry customer into a satisfied one,' write Bowen and Lawler. 'This is particularly valuable when there is little time to refer to a higher authority.'

Quicker responses to dissatisfied customers during service recovery

Solving a problem on the spot, rather than waiting for a manager to appear, can turn a dissatisfied customer into a loyal one. Many service organizations find empowering front-line staff can save them money because customers whose problems are solved quickly are generally satisfied with a smaller compensation than customers who have been further inconvenienced by having to wait for a management decision. At

Avis Rent-a-Car, management discovered that empowering front-line employees to deal with complaints and even to hand out compensation for mistakes in service, rather than asking customers to wait for a written response from head office, saved the company money and helped retain customers.

Empowered employees can be a great source of service ideas, word-of-mouth advertising and customer retention

When Crest Hotels embarked on a hospitality programme which involved training staff to be more friendly and attentive to guests, the trainers started by asking hotel managers how they thought guests viewed the service at their hotel. The managers' answers were mainly product-focused – they thought customers were concerned about things like cutlery, sheets and the size of food portions, because these were the areas that senior management tended to concentrate on. The managers were then asked to devise a checklist judging the quality of hospitality at bars and restaurants, and were each given £50 to try out the checklist on an eating establishment of their choice. They all reported that they had found the service to be appalling. Interestingly, most of them added that they feared the results would be just as bad in Crest Hotels.

Many of the managers were so taken aback by the outcome of their informal surveys that they put their heads of departments through the same awareness-raising exercise. As David Robinson, a consultant who worked with Crest developing and implementing the project, reports, 'the process worked well and the heads came up with some outstanding ideas on how to improve their own areas of responsibility.'

John Seddon, an occupational psychologist with Vanguard Consulting, argues that good service staff should be highly critical of their own employers. 'I don't mean that companies should want their employees to be stroppy or obstructive,' he says. 'Simply that they should be encouraged to challenge anything about their job that diminishes the organization's ability to serve customers by the most efficient means.'[3]

166 THE POWER OF EMPOWERMENT

Employees feel better about their jobs and themselves

Fashion retailer Laura Ashley ran a successful experiment in allowing sales assistants to ignore highly paid merchandisers and run their own shops. Staff at ten stores spent four months deciding how to market the clothes, running their own fashion shows and making changes within the shops to try to improve profits. Head office provided cash incentives linked to percentage increases and set profit targets.

According to *The Times*, the Oxford Street store increased profits by 62 per cent, one in Liverpool by 139 per cent. 'It was fun and did wonders for staff motivation,' says one manager. Managing director Steve Cotter says: 'The test proved highly successful and proved staff react quickly and effectively when given the freedom to make commercial decisions.'

There are, however, a number of costs to empowering service employees:

Empowered staff generally need more training than those who follow strict procedures

If they are to make informed decisions about what is best for both the company and the customers, they will need to have a solid understanding about the objectives and workings of the organization.

Empowered staff cost more to employ

Many service organizations rely on part-time, temporary or seasonal staff. They may need to change that profile to better-paid, full-time, permanent staff to make the investment in training worthwhile – yet this is directly opposed to current trends in a number of sectors, particularly retailing, where the move from full-time to part-time employment is accelerating.

Empowered staff may provide slow or inconsistent service delivery

Service staff paying particular attention to the needs of one customer may delay the process for others who are waiting.

'Customers value speed, and "no surprises" service delivery,' write Bowen and Lawler. 'They like to know what to expect when they revisit a service business or patronize different outlets of a franchise, but when service delivery is left to employee discretion, it may be inconsistent.'

Certain customers are looking for cheap, quick, reliable service. They do want quality but they are not necessarily expecting tender loving care. Even if they wanted it they wouldn't pay for it.

One convenience store chain actually lost customers as a result of empowering its staff. Customers wanted speed, and friendly clerks slowed things down. The fast food chain Taco Bell, on the other hand, is looking to gain an edge in the unempowered end of the market. As more fast food chains move to customized service oriented operations, Taco Bell expect to have more opportunities in the fast, low-price market niche.

Some organizations have a mix of customers, some of whom demand quick, no-frills service, while others want personal attention. Selfridges Food Halls, for example, have identified three very distinct customer types: customers who use the store as their local shop and want personal attention; lunch-time and after-work shoppers who demand speed and convenience; and 'tourist' shoppers who shop for the experience and the chance to see and buy goods they cannot find elsewhere. Satisfying the needs of all three groups takes a good deal of planning in terms of lay-out, display and flexibility of staff. Selfridges discovered that dictating to employees how to serve customers would not work in this situation, and that empowering staff to make their own decisions about how to serve each type of customer was the only way to please all of them.

Empowered staff may violate customers' perceptions of fair play

'Many customers associate sticking to procedures with being treated fairly,' write Bowen and Lawler. Customers may be more likely to return to a business if they believe that their complaint was handled effectively because of company policies, rather than because they were lucky enough to get a particular employee.

HOW TO CREATE AN EMPOWERED SERVICE ORGANIZATION

Creating an empowered service organization requires that the company examine how it tackles five areas of management:

❑ goals

❑ management attitudes

❑ training and development

❑ selection and recruitment

❑ structures and systems.

Setting goals

What is empowerment meant to accomplish? 'It is important for the general manager and executive committee to decide what specific goals they would like to achieve by implementing employee empowerment,' advises Robert Brymer of Florida State University. 'These goals must be specific, measurable and achievable. For example: In one year the hotel will have a 50 per cent improvement in guest satisfaction as measured by corporate standards.' Otherwise, empowerment can easily become something to simply 'try out for a year'.

Changing management roles and attitudes

According to Donald Laurie, founder and chief executive of Laurie International, a London-based management consultancy specializing in customer responsiveness:

> The people on the front line understand the customers' expectations and the factors that inhibit them from meeting their expectations better than any manager in the company. And it is more important for management to listen to these people than almost any other activity they perform. Yet to my continued amazement many top managers don't seem to respect the people on their front line. They fail to recognize that one of

their prime responsibilities is to acknowledge and make legitimate the problems facing front-line people, so that they can be resolved.[4]

Often the biggest problem facing people at the front line, he adds:

is that they lack the trust and support of top management and thus don't feel that they have authority to act. Without that, they are not able to take responsibility for meeting the needs of their customers, particularly where the solution to the customer problem falls outside their area of responsibility.

The company's structure, then, must change to one where:

❑ the customers define their expectations

❑ the people on the front line determine what inhibits them from meeting those expectations

❑ managers support the front line by removing any inhibitors.

Managers, says Laurie, must change their role from dictating how service is to be carried out, to removing the barriers that prevent staff from doing it themselves. He advises:

Recognize that the only people who can really meet customer requirements are those on the front line. Show them their potential, trust them, support them with the tools and training that they need, and strive to remove the factors that inhibit them. They will reward you with the financial results.

Training and development

In a detailed survey carried out by one of the authors into what actually happened in customer care programmes, one of the most disturbing results was how little customer care training was given at all levels. Little more than a quarter of companies trained top management in service quality issues, and only 40 per cent trained middle and junior managers. At the operator level, two out of three companies provided two days or less of training, and 18 per cent provided less than half a day.[5]

The implication of this relatively low level of investment is that many front-line staff are expected to deliver high levels of service quality without the skills to do so or the knowledge of what they are trying to achieve.

Both experienced and newly hired employees will need training to help them in their new roles. Their needs, however are quite different from one another. According to Brymer,

> experienced employees usually have more difficulty initially accepting decision-making responsibility. That is because they are accustomed to reverse delegation, which means passing problems to their boss or perhaps to another department. However, once they've made the transition and have accepted empowerment, they can rely on their operations experience to help them make informed decisions. They will be knowledgeable about what to do and where to turn in resolving a customer problem.
>
> Newly hired employees, on the other hand, will usually have the reverse reaction. They will accept bottom-up decision-making much more readily, taking on customer problems with a fresh and energetic approach. Their inexperience with the operation and in dealing with guests, however, will sometimes require that the newly hired employees seek advice on what to do (or be corrected after the fact).[6]

Selection and recruitment

A growing number of service managers are finding it far easier – and more effective – to recruit naturally service-minded people than to try to train staff whose personalities do not lean that way. 'Companies are moving away from blanket training – partly because it's too expensive – and are starting to use competency-based recruitment as an alternative,' says Michael Douglas, a partner at PA Consulting Group.

One of the first British companies to take this approach was Allied Lyons Retailing, which since 1984 has used psychometric testing to seek out service orientation in potential pub managers and staff. David Frean, a management development executive responsible for selection technology at Allied Lyons, says:

We use a structured interview, asking open-ended questions about people's likes, dislikes and attitudes to identify the applicant's life themes – their approaches to various aspects of the job. People who have service orientation among their life themes get genuine pleasure from doing things for other people; they get a kick out of providing good service. You could never teach that.

An internal survey found that managers recommended by the test had increased their pub's profitability by an average of 30 per cent and sales by 11 per cent, in a year. Those not recommended had increased profitability and sales by 11 and 2 per cent respectively. 'Now we don't even hire people who are not recommended by the test,' Frean says.

This idea, that attitudes matter, is now affecting even the most technical of jobs. British Gas North Thames' annual intake of apprentices was, until this year, tested only for verbal, mechanical and numerical reasoning. Customer orientation was taken into account, says Jim Needham, regional personnel services manager, but it wasn't tested for.

A pilot project will change that. Needham says:

We analysed what made the difference between a successful and a less successful candidate and boiled it down to six key competencies, including initiative, problem solving skills and customer orientation. Technical skills are still important, but now we will also look at whether the applicant will have the ability, when qualified, to act as an ambassador for the company.

According to Karen Ward, a resourcing consultant at PA Consulting Group, competency-based recruiting can help to cut through traditional stereotypes. 'One client had a fairly typical customer service staff: female and under 35. Management felt that other types, such as mature men, weren't quite suitable for customer service jobs,' she says.

After they started to recruit using tests and exercises that left little room for subjectivity, the staff profile changed. 'It is now 50:50 male:female and aged up to 55,' Ward explains.

The average educational qualifications came down, but the quality of service has increased.

More and more companies are recognizing that, in a lot of front-line jobs, it is innate traits, work style and behaviour, more than experience, educational qualification or technical abilities that differentiate between the successful and the unsuccessful performers. After all, you can always teach the technical skills, but how can you train someone to smile?

Give front-line staff the information they need

The company must ensure there are good lines of communication all the way from the front line to top management and back again. The front line should have the same information about customer's expectations and of customers' perception of their performance as top management.

Hotels, for example, can use database technology to tell front-line staff in advance where customers like their rooms to be, what newspapers they read, what special facilities they need, and the like.

Make sure someone owns the problem

Whoever first hears a customer complaint must own the problem, even if the complaint involves another department. For example, if a hotel guest in the bar explains that his laundry had not come back on time, it would be the responsibility of the bartender to ask the guest if anything had been done to correct the problem. If nothing has been done, the bartender, who now owns the problem, would have to make sure that the housekeeping department knew about the late laundry.

According to Brymer, employees at Ritz Carlton hotels are taught the following rules:[7]

☐ any employee who receives a guest complaint owns that complaint

☐ instant guest pacification will be ensured by all

☐ respond to guest wishes within ten minutes or so after the request

☐ follow up with a telephone call within 20 minutes to ensure their satisfaction.

Although the person who first hears about the problem should 'own' it to the extent of ensuring it is solved to the customer's satisfaction, it can be difficult to allocate responsibility for actually carrying out the solution. In deciding where responsibility should lie, consider:

❑ Who would the customer want to deal with this issue? For example, while a receptionist may be perfectly capable of dealing with the problem, the customer may feel better served if the problem is dealt with by someone with more status.

❑ What would be the impact of not giving the problem to the right person?

❑ How capable are the people at the front line to deal with this issue? Would they become capable with more training, experience or technical support?

❑ Who actually has to do the work?

❑ Who actually has to put things right if they go wrong?

Allow people to make mistakes

According to Brymer,

> employees who are reprimanded or criticized for making decisions that are not consistent with what the boss might have done will be very reluctant ever to make a decision again. This is not to say employees shouldn't be corrected and instructed on how to handle a situation better or that giving employees the freedom to make mistakes is tantamount to institutionalizing incompetence. But it's important that they be praised for taking the initiative and making a decision for the sake of customer service and satisfaction.

Consultant David Laurie tells of a conversation he once had with a reservation agent who had been with British Airways for one year and with an American carrier for seven years before that. 'What makes the total service experience with British Airways superior to many other airlines?' asked Laurie. She said:

The first day I joined BA my boss said, 'Do something. Don't be afraid to make a mistake, and always come down on the side of the passenger. You'll never be reprimanded for that kind of action.' I never have been. In contrast, my previous employer also gave great training. But they emphasized that you had to stick to the regulations. They created an attitude that if you didn't you would be fined or penalized in some way. It's a pity, all that good training gone to waste.

The difference between the agent's two employers was that one, BA, had managed to align its employees' emotional drives with its own needs, so that staff genuinely wanted to provide excellent service. It had then gone on to give them the tools and support they needed to do so.

This, as the following three case studies show, is what makes the difference between a genuinely empowered service organization, and a superficially empowered one.

CASE STUDIES

In the service sector, perhaps even more so than in manufacturing, there is no recipe for empowerment. What works, what doesn't, and what may be safely attempted depend on each organization's starting point, its objectives, its customer base, and its staff.

Two very different service organizations – a front-runner in the intensely competitive car rental market and a global hotel chain that once based its success on rigid conformity – have each adopted their own versions of front-line empowerment, with varying degrees of success. If they have one thing in common, it is, perhaps, the ability to capture the emotional involvement of their staff.

Avis Rent-A-Car

Avis Rent-A-Car, one of the first service companies in Britain to introduce the idea of empowering the front line, discovered some time ago that the costs of dealing with complaints letters was out of all proportion to the transactions involved.

There were hidden costs, too. The delay between the time the customer's problem occurred and the time his or her letter was answered was so long that even a generous recompense from the company was unlikely to bring them back again.

Then an Avis manager had a brainwave. The majority of complaints came to the counter clerks first. Would it not be cheaper, he suggested, if all those problems could be sorted out there? It meant, of course, giving each counter clerk the authority to satisfy customers, according to their own judgement.

The risks, on the surface, were high. Would the employees simply give away cash or vehicle upgrades for a peaceful life? Or would they forget that the purpose of the exercise was to get the customer to use Avis again?

In practice, the scheme has worked extremely well. Not only has it saved the company money, in spite of the greater volume of on-the-spot hand-outs; but the proportion of unhappy customers who have been turned into appreciative and loyal customers has dramatically increased. Moreover, the staff themselves have responded well because of the knowledge that the company puts such trust in them.

Novotel

Novotel, one of the world's largest hotel chains, is one company that made its name – and its fortune – with strict uniformity. Until 1993, every aspect of its service, from the coffee shop pie portions to the number of pillows on a bed, was decided, for all 270 hotels around the world, at head office in Paris. The rules applied whether the outside reality was a French airport, a British motorway, or an African market-place.

'The Novotel concept is based on a simple idea: consistency in room design and in the quality of the amenities from one Novotel to the next,' says Novotel's UK sales and marketing director Guy Parsons. 'Because the chain grew so quickly – at one point we were opening a hotel every fortnight – we had to bring in a structure that would help maintain and guarantee consistency.'

That structure, though largely responsible for the chain's success, did get to be stifling, he says.

Procedures were so tightly defined that if, for example, one location had a lot of Japanese customers, the local managers were simply not permitted to serve Japanese tea. We had so much conformity that we weren't responding as much as we would like to individual markets, clients or locations.

We felt it was time to free up managers to respond to individual customer's needs, and to remind them that the most important person is not their boss and his rule books, but their clients.

A programme, called 'Back to the Future', involves the adoption of a new management style and the empowerment of general managers – now called *Maitres de Maison* – and staff as a way to improve customer service.

'The first thing we did was take out layers of management,' says Parsons.

Now all parts of the company, including head office, hotels, and even the kitchens, each operate with three rather than multiple levels of management. Headquarters' departments act as consultants, advising, rather than directing, the hotels and hotel managers and, to a lesser extent, staff, have the discretion to respond to individual customer needs.

'If a regular customer always wants five pillows on his bed, hotel staff can now put them there. Before, company policy dictated that there were to be two pillows on the bed and the rest in the cupboard and there was to be no deviation. If a restaurant has a different clientele, it is now free to bring in a different menu, says Parsons.

'Some of our clients have definitely noticed changes already. They get their problems sorted out on the front line. They are not being bounced around to managers.'

Core aspects of the brand, however, such as 24 square metre bedrooms, desks in the rooms, buffet breakfasts, bilingual staff, strict pricing policies and restaurants open 6 am to midnight, will not change, he says. 'You will still be able to recognize that it's a Novotel wherever you go.'

CONCLUSION

Service organizations have both more to gain and more to lose from empowerment than manufacturing organizations. They also face a more pressing need to empower. In an increasingly competitive service sector, empowerment, and the greater customer responsiveness it can bring, is for many service organizations the best and quickest way to gain a competitive advantage.

Yet in the service sector there is no 'way to empower' any more than there is a 'way to serve'. From Avis's flexible empowerment, where counter clerks are empowered to do what they have to do to satisfy the customer, to Novotel's structured approach, where head office regulations have been only somewhat loosened, empowerment in the service sector must be redefined for every organization.

A few points will help to define what level of empowerment is best for your organization:

❑ Start from the viewpoint of the customer. The things that cause most problems for the customer are the obvious priorities for empowerment.

❑ At what point in the organization are customer needs best met, or a problem best resolved? The answer may not rest just in efficiency terms, as the Avis example shows. It may also be important to consider the best time to resolve a problem.

❑ Having decided who should own the decision, what authority do they need to carry it out? And what support do they need in terms of resources, information and training?

❑ Do not use empowerment as a way of dumping on your front-line staff the inefficiencies in your service delivery systems. Perpetual recovery quickly leads to burn-out.

Avoiding burn-out is one of the objectives of the next chapter – a guide to empowering yourself.

References

1. Bowen, D.E., and Lawler, E.E., 'The empowerment of service workers: what, why, how and when', *Sloan Management Review*, Spring 1992, Volume 33, No. 3.

2. Brymer, R.A., 'Employee empowerment: a guest-driven leadership strategy', *The Cornell HRA Quarterly*, May 1991.

3. Dearlove, D., 'Shout if you see it's wrong', *The Times*, 25 November 1993.

4. Laurie, D., *Managing the Customer Revolution*, Laurie International, 1993.

5. Clutterbuck, D. and Kernaghan, S., *Making Customers Count*, Mercury Books: London, 1991.

6. Brymer, op. cit.

7. Brymer, op. cit.

8
EMPOWERING YOURSELF

There is dignity in work only when it is work freely accepted.

Albert Camus

Empowerment is not a verb. 'You' cannot empower 'me'. It is more a state of mind and a way of working.

Ken Gilliver, head of management development and training, Ciba UK

Make every decision as if you owned the whole company

Robert Townsend, former CEO, Avis

In Chapter 1 we looked briefly at what is probably the most fundamental truth about empowerment: no one can be empowered by another person; individuals must empower themselves.

But how can a solitary person empower him or herself? Even in a flat, democratic, 'empowering' organization, complete with supportive management, high expectations and good training opportunities, empowering oneself represents a complete about-face in the way most people think about their working lives. If people in these organizations find it difficult, how can the majority, facing antiquated hierarchies, management resistance and political infighting attempt to empower themselves?

This leads us to the second fundamental truth about empowerment. Regardless of the circumstances, empowering yourself is neither easy, not quick. It calls for some fundamental changes – though of course the degree of change needed will depend on an individual's starting point – in attitudes and behaviours, communication styles, and even one's self-image.

What then are you aiming for? What does an empowered person look like? 'Empowered people,' according to Graham Oddey, an executive consultant with KPMG Peat Marwick,

> are confident and assertive. They don't need supervision. They are willing, able and highly motivated. Empowered people challenge their bosses, they also tend to be tenacious. Empowered people are energetic. They enjoy themselves and their effectiveness means their bosses have more time to devote to bigger issues, and are not bogged down in a mire of irritating little problems which their staff really ought to be able to fix themselves.[1]

BA chairman Sir Colin Marshall, in describing his basic requirements of a good manager, adds to the picture of an empowered individual. He or she:

❑ has lots of energy

❑ is totally willing to commit him or herself emotionally

❑ has a desire to excel

❑ has the ability to take delight from the successes of others

❑ has a genuine liking for people

❑ has a good self-image

❑ appreciates, but is not dominated by, the need for analysis

❑ believes in the ultimate business efficacy of probity – that being truthful pays off

❑ has a usefully alert and curious mind with a fair degree of common sense.[2]

Pulling together observations and comments from a variety of sources, we can posit that most truly empowered people, whether they be machine operators, check out clerks or chief executives, will have some or all of the following characteristics. They are:

❑ well trained

❑ confident

❑ enthusiastic, motivated and committed

❑ able to use their natural creativity

❑ able to take responsibility

❑ able to communicate needs, successes, problems and ideas

❑ able to work on their own or in a team

❑ flexible, both in what they do and how they tackle new situations

❑ able to make decisions when needed, but know when to involve others

❑ proud of their work

❑ proud of their team and their organization

❑ trusting of and trusted by colleagues

❑ comfortable about questioning the status quo

❑ able to understand the context and consequences of their work

❑ able to set their own priorities and manage themselves

❑ able to make process improvements at their own initiative

❑ knowledgeable about how well they are performing

❑ clear about who their customers (internal or external) are, and what they require of them.

❑ empowered outside the workplace as well

❑ still learning and developing.

HOW TO BECOME AN EMPOWERED PERSON

Recognizing an empowered person is one thing, becoming one is quite another. To become empowered, then, an individual needs to:

❑ develop the skills needed to take responsibility

❑ take responsibility

❑ share responsibility

❑ develop effective networks of information and influence

❑ help others in their team to acquire the personal skills they need to be effective

❑ enhance personal and team creativity

❑ find ways to make a difference

❑ be prepared to challenge the accepted wisdom

❑ take responsibility not just for his or her own job, but for his or her career

❑ maintain a healthy balance between work and personal life

❑ do a job he or she enjoys

❑ keep learning.

Take responsibility

An individual can take responsibility at several levels:

❑ for tasks directly allocated to him or her alone

❑ for tasks allocated to a group of people in general – for example, whoever is nearest an unattended phone is the person responsible for answering it and for ensuring that the enquiry is dealt with properly

❑ for tasks that aren't allocated to anyone, but which clearly need attending to – for example, a badly packaged parcel, another employee in distress, or a misdirected visitor

❑ for tasks that haven't yet been conceived, such as developing and piloting a new and better system, or improving a product.

A fully empowered person takes responsibility at all these levels and doesn't normally need to think twice about doing so. Reaching that point, however, takes time and effort. Douglas Paul, a management consultant working with the NHS Perth and Kinross Unit, is helping to move management at this NHS trust towards empowerment. As he sees it, an individual's empowerment comes in three stages, akin to the growth of a child:

1. **Dependence**: a hierarchical dependence on orders.

2. **Independence**: when an individual is able to take decisions alone. At this stage he or she gains confidence, becomes rebellious and tests the limits of their empowerment.

3. **Interdependence**: an individual discovers that no man is an island, and learns a new sort of dependence based on equality, cooperation and trust in co-workers.

Develop the skills necessary to take responsibility

A number of skills are necessary to reach the point of interdependence.

Develop trust in your colleagues, and help them develop trust in you

How much do your boss and your colleagues trust you? Trust is an essential element in feeling that you can delegate to someone else. There are three basic components of trust in a professional relationship:

❑ trust in each other's integrity and goodwill

❑ trust that you share common objectives, or are open about conflicting objectives

❑ trust in each other's competence to do what you promise.

Understand your strengths, weaknesses and limits

An empowered person seeks, through formal and informal appraisals, from managers, colleagues and subordinates, to understand his or her strengths and weaknesses. They also seek for themselves the resources they need to build on their weaknesses and develop their strengths.

184 THE POWER OF EMPOWERMENT

Ask yourself:

❑ What do you lack confidence in your ability to do? Do you
   lack confidence because of a real, or an imagined, lack of
   experience or ability? Any lack of confidence in an area
   of your job will be a potential or actual limitation on your
   ability to take responsibility. As an empowered person
   you will look to gain the needed confidence.

❑ What do other people see as your strengths and weaknesses?
      Are they right, even if only to a certain extent? Are
   they wrong, and thus limiting your opportunities with
   misconceptions about your abilities? What can you do to
   change those perceptions?
      Try building other people's confidence in you bit by bit,
   showing first that you can handle responsibility for tasks
   with small risks and gradually extending the boundaries
   of your perceived capability.

❑ Do you face problems at work that are genuinely beyond
   your level? Do you know where to seek help? If so, do you
   seek it? Empowered people know their limits, know
   where to find help, and have no qualms about asking for
   it when necessary.

Self-knowledge is a strength. In an empowered organization,
employees should be able to get information about their own
strengths, weaknesses and performance from 360 degree
appraisals – evaluations by their peers, direct reports, bosses, internal, and in some cases, external, customers.
   Even in an unempowered organization, empowered people
seek this information for themselves, asking those around
them: 'How do I help you do your job? How do I hinder your
effectiveness?' Armed with this knowledge, an individual can
set personal improvement goals and make a more substantial
contribution.

*Try to see your job in the context of the business, and not just your
part of it.*

How does your job fit in with others? What is its real purpose? This is not necessarily what the job description says,

nor what the specific job elements are.

Do you understand the jobs of the people working around you? If you do, you can make a much wider contribution and approach your job in a way that will best help them.

Are there responsibility gaps in your organization? Is there a significant issue, relating to service delivery, product quality or cost control, which should be, but isn't, at the top or near the top of someone else's list? Can you do anything about it?

Develop the confidence and self-image that allows you to take responsibility

Confidence and self-image create some of the strongest motivation, and some of the most powerful limitations, to any attempt to change behaviour. People do what they believe they are capable of doing, and it can take a significant effort to overcome one's personal view of one's capabilities.

The issue is perhaps most familiar in sport, with the concept of the psychological barrier. The four-minute mile was vastly more difficult for sprinters to crack than the three minute 57 second mile, because of the psychological barrier it presented. Similarly, a secretary who sees herself as 'only a typist' will have a great deal more difficulty taking on administrative responsibilities than one in the same position, with the same abilities, whose self-image is that of a management trainee.

Empowered people challenge, constantly, their own beliefs about what they are and are not capable of.

Steve Dyer, a process operator, was among the first hourly paid people at Walkers Smiths Snack Foods' Swansea factory to take the company's course on empowering behaviours. 'It has changed the way that I work,' he says. 'The biggest change, though, was in my own self-esteem. The course has given me the confidence to get more involved and gave me some skills in how to handle people better.'

Share power and responsibility

Sharing a problem may halve it, but it also doubles the authority and influence you have in dealing with it, if those with whom you share it are also committed to the same goals and there is a strong fund of organizational and personal goodwill.

By the same token, releasing power to others serves to empower you more. Power held tight by one individual is like the genie in the lamp. It's not much use while it's locked away and if you do decide to use it you may find you only have a limited number of wishes before it's taken away from you.

As a broad rule, every manager should be sharing out at least 25 per cent of his or her job each year, by:

❑ delegating responsibility to people who have been coached to take it

❑ systematizing processes so that they no longer need the same level of judgemental input and managerial control.

Develop effective networks of information and influence

This was dealt with in greater depth in Chapter 6, but suffice to say that empowered people know how to find out what they need to know to get things done. They do not wait for memos to arrive, but seek out the formal and informal information networks in the company to get the information they need to get things done.

Nor do they keep to themselves such information, and the power it represents. Harvard Business School's Judith Rosener, in a study of empowering management style among female executives, found that: 'While many leaders see information as power and thus as a limited commodity to be coveted, [empowered people] are comfortable letting power and information change hands.'[3]

Sharing power and information accomplishes several things, she says:

It creates loyalty by letting subordinates know they are trusted and their ideas respected. It sets an example and can enhance the general communication flow, and it helps ensure leaders will hear about problems before they explode. It also gives employees what they need to solve problems and see the reasoning behind decisions.

Rosener's interviewees primed the information flow in a variety of ways, such as encouraging others to have a say in almost every aspect of work; using a conversational style that sends signals inviting people to get involved; confirming that they really are including people's opinions by asking for suggestions before they reach their own conclusions; and testing particular decisions with others before implementing them.

As one of Rosener's interviewees described it: 'When I face a tough decision, I always ask my employees, "What would you do if you were me?" This approach generates good ideas and introduces my employees to the complexity of management decisions.'

Empowered people, says Rosener,

> use participation to clarify their own views and to ensure that they haven't overlooked an important consideration. They find that participation increases both the amount of information available to them and support for the decisions ultimately reached. It also ensures they are more likely to know ahead of time who is likely to oppose their views.

There are, however, disadvantages to sharing information, adds Rosener:

> Soliciting ideas and information from others takes time, often requires giving up some control, opens the door to criticism, and exposes personal and turf conflicts. People may reject or challenge what the leader has to say; employees may become frustrated when their ideas are solicited but not used; and, because information is a form of power, bosses who share it may be seen as weak or naive. Asking for ideas and information can be interpreted as not having the answers.

Empowered people keep information flowing in all directions, to and from subordinates, colleagues – and managers.

Thomas Kempner, Emeritus Professor of Management Studies at Henley Management College, offers some advice, from the boss's point of view, about how a subordinate can best handle the tricky issue of upward communication:[4]

❑ Please do not give me nasty surprises. I should not have to say 'You should have told me about this before.'

❑ Do not cover up problems until it is too late for careful thought and action, and can be dealt with only by fire fighting.

❑ It is not helpful to be told: 'We must have an immediate decision on this', when you should have prepared the ground weeks ago.

❑ Please do not send me only memos or copies of letters showing how clever you have been.

❑ Prepare your case carefully before we meet. Give me the alternative to any plan of action, not just the one you favour. Partial advice will be remembered the next time.

❑ If you want an answer to a complex issue – and you should not have to bother me with anything else – let me have details in advance. It is unreasonable to expect an instant reply on difficult issues or figures off the cuff.

❑ Press your views hard but, once the decision is made, carry it out as though it is your own, even when you do not agree with it. One day, when you have my job, you will expect no less from your staff.

❑ Be positive and offer solutions to problems. Those who are forever whining about their difficulties are rather depressing. They do not improve my day.

❑ Be brief. I have a lot of other problems, so please try not to be one of them.

Empowered people also build their influencing skills so they can better sell their ideas. Presentation skills, in particular, are vital in ensuring that your voice is heard on the issues you want to influence.

Help others in your teams acquire the skills they need to be effective.

You need teams to get things done – time spent supporting other team members is usually time well spent, as mutual support and advice will help raise the performance of the whole team.

Supporting team members involves not just sharing skills and information, though. It also involves building the self-esteem of others, inspiring them, and giving credit where credit is due. Building others' self-esteem is an important part of teamworking, says Walkers Smiths' Steve Dyer:

> The way you talk to someone can affect the way you solve a problem; the way you answer a question can make or break them; and really listening to people helps to encourage them. But if someone has a problem you don't want to go down there and immediately take over. You should just be available to offer help if needed.

Supporting your team also involves inspiring and energizing them. As one of Rosener's interviewees told her: 'Getting people excited is an important way to influence those you have no control over.'

Empowered people also give others credit and praise and send signals of recognition. After all, the more generous you are in recognizing the part other people had to play in your successes, the more likely you are to be invited to play in their game too.

Enhance personal and team creativity

Empowered people know how to draw on their own, and their team's creativity to help solve problems and make process improvements. They are not, as so many people are, hampered by misconceptions about creativity.

'Creativity has very little to do with colour swatches and drawing boards, and a lot to do with improving effectiveness at work,' says Elizabeth Rogers, a UK management consultant specializing in creativity:

> People often think they are not creative because they have

trouble, say, drawing or writing poetry. But everyone has opinions, and anyone with opinions about problems can come up with ideas to help solve them.

People tend to categorize themselves as being either analytical or creative. But we can all use both skills to some extent. We also tend to underestimate how much hard analytical thinking goes into generating new ideas. It's a popular belief that creative, intuitive people do not use logic; that their ideas come from sudden flashes of insight. Yet most of those hunches and brainstorms are born of a long process of observation and analysis.

Rogers describes a typical scenario: a staff member expresses an opinion about a work issue, and her manager responds aggressively: 'OK. How do you think we should do things differently?'

'Staff should take up that challenge,' says Rogers. 'We all have a duty to ourselves and our colleagues to come up with ideas about how things should be done better.'

Unfortunately, the work environment doesn't always make that easy. A recent study at Ford of Europe revealed that creativity among employees is inhibited unless organizational structures are set up not only to make creativity possible but to nurture it as well.[5]

'Managers must actively encourage people to come forward with ideas – even radical, half-formed, or not quite relevant ones,' says Rogers. They also have to stop knocking ideas on the head with such killer phrases as: 'We haven't got the budget', 'That's not a priority right now', or 'Why don't you go away and write a report about it?'. 'Companies also need a good system of internal communication to channel ideas to the people best able to act on them,' she adds.

Some organizations point to intrapreneurship, the idea of creating an entrepreneurial atmosphere inside a corporation to seize ideas and opportunities originated within, as a way to harness their internal creative resources. However, Jack Matson, of the Cullen College of Engineering at the University of Houston, has found that intrapreneurship often doesn't work.[6]

Bureaucratic structures fulfil the purpose of efficiently delivering a company's products and services. The more efficient the

structure is, the greater the profit. Conversely, entrepreneurship (and, for the same reasons, intrapreneurship) is inefficient. Creative ideas usually do not pan out. Entrepreneurs
know they are playing the odds, and only a small percentage
of their ideas survive in the marketplace. Intrapreneurship
would mean empowering creative people and relaxing management controls, but these changes are anathema to strong
corporate cultures.

'Skunkworks' are one way to allow the spirit of creativity to
flow within a corporate culture. The term, coined by management consultant and coiner of buzzwords, Tom Peters,
describes the breakthrough products and solutions that
come, not from corporate R&D labs, but from creative misfits
in another department, often working with improvised equipment, in their own time and without official sanction. The
personal interest that goes into these projects means that
they can, and do, work against the odds. But, warns Peter
Martin, author of *How To Survive and Prosper in a Recession*,
'just because you are a cantankerous misfit and your office is
a dump, it does not necessarily mean you are a genius in a
skunkworks.'[7]

Find ways to make a difference

You can make a difference to your team or organization's
effectiveness either through the responsibilities assigned to
you in your job, through a task force outside your job, or
through your personal qualities, such as creativity or an ability
to inspire others. An analysis of your strengths, weaknesses
and talents, together with an understanding of your organization's needs, can help you pinpoint these areas.

Are you making a difference? Martin suggests a quick acid
test: 'Would an outsider looking at you and your colleagues
decide that what you do is essential to the survival of the
organization? How would what the customer buys be harmed
if your job did not exist?'[8]

For many people, the answers would be 'no' and 'not
much' respectively. There are, however, ways people in any
job can change their approach to really make a difference.

Martin suggests:

- **Get closer to the customers**: find ways of tying your job more closely to the end-product your company provides. If you are in R&D, can you regularly put aside some time to spend with customers, answering their queries and picking their brains? If you are in accounts, can you make the tasks of the production department easier?

- **Identify new markets**: every time you get a customer complaint, think of ways of turning that complaint into an opportunity.

- **Provide valuable data**: find way of putting what you know about the company and its customers into data the whole company can benefit from.

- **Make the data you already provide more relevant**: redesign the data collection and processing you do, as far as possible, to get at what the recipients really want to know rather than what is convenient to provide.

- **Replace an outside supplier**: if you are already providing a service to one department, could you provide the same service to someone else, at no additional cost?

- **Find solutions to problems**: bosses get tired of hearing about problems. Get a reputation for your department or yourself as provider of solutions rather than problems.[9]

Be prepared to challenge the accepted wisdom

Empowered people question, argue and disagree when necessary. They stand their ground – not to be bloody-minded, but to arrive at the best solution. They shout when something is wrong, they know the difference between consensus and acquiescence, and they can smell groupthink at 60 paces. Unempowered people, on the other hand, prefer to agree with the boss and the experts, however wrong they may be. The Bay of Pigs fiasco, the disastrous launch of New Coke, and the design of Ford Pintos have all been traced back to team members who, despite their better judgement, chose to agree with the group, the boss and the experts.

John Seddon, an occupational psychologist with Vanguard Consulting, argues that

> real change can only occur if people are empowered to thump the table and refuse to put up with the less efficient way of doing tasks, and when employees regard it as a fundamental part of their job to question why the tasks they perform are organized in the way they are. Such behaviour, however, is traditionally resisted by managers, partly because they do not have answers to questions; because they do not want staff to know they do not have the power to authorize changes; or because they feel their role is at risk if ideas for improvements are accepted from 'below'.[10]

Some, however, are prepared to take the risk. At Frizzell Financial Services there are 'silly boards' dotted around the office on which anyone can list tasks which in their view could be changed or eradicated. Teams have come up with some highly effective ideas over the year which they have researched and implemented.[11]

At Harvester Restaurants, making staff teams responsible for meeting their own sales targets led to apparently unreasonable behaviour on the part of Duncan Podmore, a grill chef at the Bulldog Harvester in Ashford, West London. To the dismay of the Bulldog's manager, Stephen Rose, Podmore's concern that his team should beat their target during the Christmas period prompted him to challenge the company's unwritten policy of not opening on Christmas Day. Rose, who admits he would have preferred to spend the day with his family, finally agreed that his reason for not opening – 'We just don't' – was inadequate. The initiative was vindicated when the Bulldog beat its target, outperforming other Harvester outlets. As a result, management canvassed staff in the other outlets and with the full support of the marketing department, all Harvester Restaurants now open on Christmas day; all because a grill chef was bold enough to suggest it.[12]

Managing and challenging your boss really amounts to managing change, assert J Kenneth Matejka, professor of management at Duquesne University in Pittsburgh, and Richard J Dunsing, director of the University of Richmond's Management Institute.

194   THE POWER OF EMPOWERMENT

You may want your boss to act differently, but he or she is not going to change unless you initiate the process. Overcoming your boss's resistance to change is the key here. Resistance is caused by misunderstanding, fear, distrust, the desire to protect the status quo, and the need to save face and preserve one's turf. Overcoming resistance is rooted in information, support, negotiation, and helping to set up new rewards that are more valuable than the current ones. Most employees know what kind of problem they have with their boss; they also know how to solve it. Nevertheless, they either hide behind the assertion that it can't be done, or they bungle their attempts to do it. That way we can ensure failure and say: 'See I told you it wouldn't work'.[13]

Take responsibility not just for your job, but for your career

Automatic career advancement is, it seems, a thing of the past. Employees in most industries can no longer expect promotions to come simply as rewards for loyalty and good performance. Flattened hierarchies and reductions in management numbers mean there simply aren't enough senior posts to offer all the deserving candidates.

According to the UK's Institute of Management, the number of upward career moves made by managers has declined by nearly 40 per cent since a peak in 1987, while downward moves have doubled since 1980. Delayering and restructuring has only exacerbated this trend, so that more and more people will hit what is known a career plateau – the point where they can go no further in an organization – earlier in their careers. Researchers at the Sundridge Park Management Centre surveyed managers on the topic in 1985, and again in 1993. According to research consultant Peter Harriet, they found that: 'whereas managers aged 45 to 50 used to realize they would not be promoted again, now they are hitting the plateau much earlier, anywhere between 30 and 40'.[14]

And, though plateauing is normally thought to apply only to managers, many talented and ambitious people are now finding even the first rung of the career ladder increasingly difficult to reach. Now plateauing can apply to anyone, from junior clerk to senior executive, who has the ability, but not the opportunity, to move up.

People whose careers have plateaued usually follow one of three paths:

❑ they become demotivated, lose interest in work and their performance and self-esteem suffers

❑ they cling to the belief that working harder, longer or smarter will eventually ensure a promotion, becoming difficult to work for and live with, and find the reality that much harder to accept when they do realize they won't be promoted

❑ they recognize the situation for what it is and deal with it.

Dealing with the career plateau is a step most people will have to take at some point in their careers. There are a number of ways to make the most of the situation:

❑ **Be realistic**: the first step in tackling a career plateau is to recognize that your career has plateaued, not because of any personal failing or lack of ability on your part, but simply because there is no longer enough room on the career ladder. And ask whether you really *have* plateaued. Perhaps you are unreasonably impatient for advancement, or haven't yet fully exploited the possibilities of your current job.

❑ **Audit your skills**: take stock of your skills; find ways to develop the ones you are weak in, by, for example, adding to your qualifications; look for ways to apply the ones you are strong in; and let your boss know how you think they can be applied.

The most important skills to focus on are the transferable ones. These skills, which can be applied in virtually any role, include teamworking, oral and written communications, listening and counselling skills, leadership, problem-solving, business awareness, setting priorities, managing time effectively, numeracy and computer literacy.

Look, too, at skills you have developed outside of work – in voluntary work, helping a family business, raising a family or recreational activities.

196 THE POWER OF EMPOWERMENT

'As well as extending one's employment horizons, such an analysis can suggest areas for self-development. A growing number of progressive employers expect staff to explore their own competencies and identify areas in which the employer can support them to develop their skills to mutual benefit,' says Chris Dunn, a career counsellor and managing director of TDS Consulting Group.[15]

❑ If there are fewer opportunities for promotion and greater responsibility by going upward, then look for a horizontal career path – opportunities to grow in the jobs you have.

For example, Drew Melton, a photocopy technician at Prospect Associates, a Maryland consultancy, chose the horizontal growth route. He started as a photocopy machine operator in 1990 and remains a photocopy machine operator today, but with vastly increased responsibilities. Two weeks after he was hired, he went to the Prospect president Laura Henderson and told her how he could run document production better and faster. She gave him carte blanche to do things his way. 'They're listening to my ideas, and that's why I'm making changes and contributing to the company,' says Melton. Today he runs a virtual Xerox fiefdom, dispensing advice to Prospect's harried consultants, who rely on his painstaking attention to detail to give their proposals a professional look. Melton hasn't climbed a corporate ladder, but he has increased his contribution to the company by honing his skills and expanding the scope of his job. His salary has increased by 40 per cent, he is respected by the company's professional staff, and there's no pressure on him to 'move up'.[16]

❑ Look for new challenges and opportunities to gain new skills and experiences outside work, perhaps through a sabbatical, or a secondment with a university, a subsidiary, or a voluntary or government organization.

Even people who don't feel they have plateaued would be advised not to settle too comfortably into one job role, writes management writer Desmond Dearlove of *The Times*:

Managers who have been in the same post for more than three years risk becoming demotivated by doing the same tasks over and over again with little opportunity for variation. If performance is not to suffer, they need to find ways to stay fresh.

Part of the problem is that manager fatigue often leads to a feeling of career stagnation and apathy, while at the same time raising stress levels. Where this is accompanied by a drop in performance, it makes the long-serving manager more vulnerable to redundancy – the very thing he or she may be trying to avoid by staying put.[17]

Maintain a healthy balance between work and personal life

Ricardo Semler, the peripatetic chief executive of Semco Brazil, found that running a rapidly changing semi-anarchic company was all very well, but it almost hospitalized him from stress-related illnesses – at the age of 25.

'Before I could reorganize Semco,' he realized,

> I had to reorganize myself. Long hours were the first issue I tackled. They are one of the biggest symptoms of time sickness, a disease that afflicts far too many executives. So I set 7 pm as the time I would leave the office, no matter what. After that, I would go to the movies, read books (but not business books) anything but work. Next I resolved to delegate furiously and to throw unneeded paper away.[18]

Semler has now recovered so completely he no longer wears a wristwatch. Most British managers, however, haven't. According to a survey by the Institute of Management, virtually all British managers work for substantially more than their contractual hours and almost half regularly clock up more than 50 hours a week. Three quarters of managers are anxious about the demands their working hours make on their family relationships and 40 per cent are actually suffering from too much work.

A graph of working hours from the beginning of the twentieth century would show managers and other employees alike working approximately 60 hours a week, spread over six days, in the year 1900. By the mid-1950s this had dropped,

on average, by around a third. The trend line for managers
and other committed professionals has been steadily uphill
again since then, however, and shows no sign of slackening
off. We are in imminent danger of splitting into two groups of
working people: Those who work 30 hours or less each week,
and thereby lose out on many of the benefits of training,
empowerment, and legislative protection; and those who
work perhaps three times as many hours, and pay the price
in terms of health and family relationships.

'It's madness really,' says Charlie Monkcom, of New Ways
to Work, a charity campaigning for flexible working hours. 'A
lot of people are working ludicrous hours while a lot of others are not in paid work at all. Something has got to give.'

Those people who do work ludicrous hours risk harming
the quality of their work. According to Shaun Tyson, professor of Human Resources Management at the Cranfield School
of Management, the inverted 'U'-curve of performance, with
fatigue and a decline in performance setting in after excessive hours, applies to managers just as it does to junior doc-
tors or air traffic controllers.

What keeps people in the office so long? Semler blames it
on the mistaken belief that effort and result are directly pro-
portional, that the quantity of work is more important than
its quality, and that if you can delegate, you can be replaced.
This, he says, is nonsense. 'If it were true that you could
establish a successful business just by arriving early and
staying late, then every mailman could be Howard Hughes,'
he argues. Yet many employers expect their managers to do
just that. As Tyson sees it: 'Junior and middle managers are
working longer hours because they are no longer the elite.
They are behaving, and being treated, much more like any
other employee – like a resource that you can buy and then
get rid of.'

Self-empowerment is the way out of this demotivating trap.
That's what the lawyers at F J White and Co discovered.
Launched four and a half years ago by a group of solicitors
who wanted more flexibility in their working lives, it is one of
the few law firms in the country staffed largely on a part-
time and flexi-time basis.

'In a traditional law practice people tend to work long

hours because it looks better. Here, it is accepted that you may have to leave at three to pick up your kids from school,' says Catrin Burton, one of F J White's solicitors.

> Though we have all worked very long hours when it's been necessary, we never stay in the office for appearance's sake. Instead we work very intensely while we are here, cut out the socializing and the pub lunches, and telescope the day. Working nine to three, you soon realize how much time is wasted in a nine to seven working day.

Do a job you enjoy

It is easier to empower yourself if you love what you do, but so often the inverse is true – empowered people enjoy their jobs.

Commonly held attitudes to work hold that most people work to pay the mortgage, or to gain power or security. Much of the work done on job motivation and empowerment, however, disputes this. Study after study shows that if the job is right, people can be powerfully motivated by the satisfaction of work itself.

Mihaly Csikszentmihalyi, a professor of psychology at the University of Chicago, found in a 1989 study of 1,000 American working people that almost a third of respondents said they had felt powerfully uplifted as though from outside in some part of the daily round. Moreover, feelings of this type arose markedly more often at work than in leisure hours, especially when the job was complex and demanding.[19]

Csikszentmihalyi found that people are at their best in every sense when they experience what he calls 'flow'. He describes it as the state in which people are so involved in an activity that nothing else seems to matter. Significantly, the bulk of flow experiences are felt at work. And, while more common at higher levels of official responsibility, they are certainly not confined there.

In his book, *Flow – The Psychology of Optimal Experience*, Csikszentmihalyi cites the case of Joe, a welder in a Chicago factory:

Joe had apparently mastered every phase of the plant's operation, and he was now able to take anyone's place if necessary. Moreover, he could fix any broken down piece of machinery, ranging from huge mechanical cranes to tiny electronic monitors. But what astounded people most was that Joe not only could perform these tasks, but actually enjoyed it when he was called on to do them.

Work that leads to flow, says the professor, is characterized by at least some of the following conditions:

❑ the task is one we are capable of completing

❑ we are able to concentrate entirely on the work in hand

❑ it has goals which are clear, although not necessarily defined in detail

❑ it provides immediate feedback

❑ it gives us a feeling of deep but effortless involvement that removes from consciousness the worries and frustrations of everyday life

❑ it allows us full control over our actions

❑ while we are actually doing it, our sense of self disappears, only to return with added strength when the task is finished

❑ It transforms our awareness of time, so that hours seemingly pass in minutes, or minutes stretch out like hours.

Flow is triggered, he says, not by things imposed from outside, such as extra pay. Rather, our drive is totally internal – the real delight of personal growth achieved by gaining more complex abilities.

Achieving the feeling of flow is a very personal matter, but the basis lies in understanding what drives you, and finding work that provides that motivation. Are you motivated by completing a complex task, using creativity to solve problems, or helping others? There are some elements of each in most jobs; build on those and try to steer your career in that direction.

It's also important to maintain your motivation where it might otherwise lag, by developing greater self-discipline, setting goals for both your job and your life, and being clear about the rewards you seek from your work – both from yourself and others.

Keep on learning

Empowered people keep learning, formally and informally, at work and in their personal activities, throughout their life. Empowered people also have an advantage over others – they know how to learn.

According to Chris Argyris of the Harvard Graduate School of Business and Education,

> any company that aspires to succeed in the tougher business environment of the 1990s must first resolve a basic dilemma: success in the marketplace increasingly depends on learning, yet most people don't know how to learn. What's more, those members of the organization that many assume to be the best at learning are, in fact, not very good at it. I am talking about the well-educated, high-powered, high-commitment professionals who occupy key leadership positions in modern corporations.[20]

The most successful people often have the most difficulty learning, says Argyris, because they have rarely experienced failure, and have thus never learned how to learn from failure. 'So, whenever their learning strategies go wrong, they become defensive, screen out criticism, and put the blame on anyone and everyone but themselves. In short, their ability to learn shuts down precisely at the moment they need it the most.'

Another problem with learning, adds Argyris, is that most people define learning too narrowly as mere problem-solving, so they focus on identifying and correcting errors in the external environment. Solving problems is important, but if learning is to persist, managers and employees must also look inwards. They need to reflect critically on their own behaviour, identify the ways they inadvertently contribute to the organization's problems, and then change how they act. In particular, they must learn how the very way they go about defining and solving problems can be a source of problems in its own right.

Consultant Milo Lynch agrees, explaining: 'Our society and education system focus on developing operative skills – skills to enable people to do things and solve problems on their own – and the opportunity to learn or acquire cooperative, or teamworking, skills have been absent from many people's experience.'

High-flying young managers in particular tend to be skilled in problem-solving and weak in teamworking skills, he maintains. They are, he adds, often promoted only to find that their ensuing performance is less impressive than anticipated. This, he says, may be because they continue problem-solving when they should be delegating problems to their subordinates.

Other learning difficulties he sees among young managers include seeing only one dimension of the problem, having short-term focus, easily seeing what is wrong, a high capability for argument and debate, and poor listening skills.

Lynch encourages these people to set purposes – why they are doing a given task – end results and success criteria:

> I emphasize developing the skills of foresight, imagination and vision. I believe these facilities to be absolutely crucial to managers, whose interests need to encompass managing the future, visualizing it and sharing that vision with their colleagues. These are all extensions of basic cooperative skills and are highly valuable to any individual. They are also necessary to be able to cooperate with others, to lead, motivate, enthuse, listen with care, tap into experience, create a common vision, recognize and exercise the talents of others, and help them to build confidence. In other words, cooperative skills are needed to enable people to empower the people they work with.

Many professionals only learn these things when forced to by a crisis, says J.B.M. Kassarjian, a Professor of Management at Babson College in Wellesley, Massachusetts:

> When asked about pivotal learning events in their career, most senior managers cite a jolting experience: an unexpected challenge, a shocking outcome, or an unanticipated failure, all of which they had to overcome. As a result, their bar of expectation was raised sharply, and sometimes tilted to new angles. They had to discover their own untested capacities through stretching hard to scale an unfamiliar barrier.[21]

Develop and follow a personal development plan

Empowered people work to overcome unfamiliar barriers by following a personal development plan.

The vehicles for doing this will vary from organization to organization. An important first step, however, is to recognize the need to develop across all aspects of your life. For example, a manager might become a world-renowned expert in his field, but fail to acquire the maturity that comes from involvements outside of work.

Our model assumes four strands of development:

1. **work**: the immediate job and its requirements for the foreseeable future

2. **career**: often, but not necessarily, the same thing

3. **family**: the work of Edgar Schein of the Alfred P. Sloan School of Management in Boston, and of other pioneers in the study of corporate bigamy indicates that family demands frequently reach their peak at the same time as work and career demands

❑ **leisure and self-fulfilment**: the need to achieve outside the work and career environment.

A significant part of the groundwork of any self-development programme is to understand and manage these conflicting demands. At the same time, it is essential to recognize why it is necessary to set personal goals and work towards them. The steps involved in designing a personal development plan include the following.

Set challenging but realistic goals

The key here is to balance enthusiasm and vision with wisdom and experience. You need to be able to:

❑ assess where you are now

❑ identify, understand and accept the reality of personal strengths and weaknesses

❑ identify development options

❏ prioritize development options within a framework of clear personal objectives.

This is an iterative process. It is hard to assess where you are now if you don't have a clear goal to measure against. At the same time, goals need to be built out of an understanding of your personal potential.

Ruth Hartley, a planning and inventory manager in the operations department at Hiram Walkers's head office in Horsham, followed the company's self-managed learning programme. She found it was more productive to set work-related, rather than general goals. 'It is better to set learning objectives that are closely linked to your job, if only because pressure of time make them more realistic.'[22]

Construct pathways

With a relatively small amount of help, most people can learn to draw development pathways – routes, via promotions or training by which they can achieve their objectives – for themselves. These pathways are not, or should not be, rigid. They begin with the priority goals and work backwards to practical actions that can be taken immediately. They also include clear milestones, which can form the basis for discussion with other people who have an interest in the individual's development.

Review your progress

Because most people find it difficult to stick to a personal improvement plan on their own, the company can help with a variety of methods of motivation and encouragement. The appraisal process is clearly important here. So, too are peer group pressure and the provision of appropriate counselling services. Above all, the company can register its approval when people achieve their individual milestones.

CONCLUSION

Empowering oneself is a challenging, and essential, aspect of any empowerment programme. The first step is recognizing that you already do have a great deal of power, regardless of your position in the organization. The trick is to develop the skills needed to harness it.

Empowering yourself should make you more effective at work, more pleasant to work for and a good deal happier. As writer, tramp, gardener, scullery boy and very empowered person, Maxim Gorky discovered: 'When work is a pleasure, life is a joy! When work is a duty, life is slavery.'

References

1.   Oddey, G., 'Take a horse to water, but ...' *Managing Service Quality*, November 1993.

2.   Marshall, C., 'Flat, not flatulent', *Management Today*, April 1990.

3.   Rosener, J.B., 'Ways women lead', *Harvard Business Review*, November/December 1990.

4.   Kempner, T., 'Guidelines to life as a subordinate', *The Times*, 23 August, 1990.

5.   McNamara, J., 'Ford's engineers become lateral thinkers', *Financial Times*, 10 May 1993.

6.   Matson, J.B., 'From entrepreneurship to intrapreneurship – the problem of organizational rejection', *MBA Update*, May 1992.

7.   Martin, P., 'How to become indispensable', *Financial Times*, 2 June 1990.

8.   Ibid.

9.   Ibid.

10. Dearlove, D., 'Shout if you see it's wrong', *The Times*, 25 November 1993.

11. Pickard, J., 'The real meaning of empowerment', *Personnel Management*, November 1993.

12. Dearlove, D., op. cit.

13. Matejka, J.K. and Dunsing, J.R., 'Managing the baffling boss', *Personnel*, February, 1989.

14. Dearlove, D., 'Rewards on the level', *The Times,* 20 January, 1994.

15. Schofield, P., 'Take ownership of your career', *The Sunday Times*, 14 November 1993.

16. Ehrenfeld, T., 'Bottoms up', *Inc,* July 1993.

17. Dearlove, D., 'Fresh steps that dodge job fatigue', *The Times,* 1 April 1993.

18. Semler, R., (1993) *Maverick!*, Century, London.

19. Dixon, M., 'The spiritual dimension of high performance', *Financial Times*, 3 April 1991.

20. Argyris, C., 'Teaching smart people how to learn', *Harvard Business Review*, May – June 1991.

21. Kassarjian, J.B.M., 'Jolt your managers out of their comfortable groove, they may learn to lead change', *Perspectives for Managers,* No. 4, 1991.

22. Cunningham, I., and Hurley, B., 'Imbibing a new way of learning', *Personnel Management*, March 1993.

9
CASE STUDIES

OTICON – THE SPAGHETTI ORGANIZATION

Oticon, one of the world's leading producers of hearing aids, has developed a radical new management and communication system: 'We are trying to get away from a command structure to a problem-solving structure. Projects, management and staff are thoroughly entangled with each other. We call it a spaghetti organization,' says Lars Kolind, Oticon's managing director.

Copenhagen-based Oticon has a fluid organizational structure that allows employees to solve problems outside their own field. 'It's integrated not structured, but it's fast and creative and it works,' says Kolind.

Oticon's first step was to take down all the partition walls which made up its office cubicles. The 130 management and staff now work in one large open room. 'In the past,' explains Kolind, 'too much energy was spent on departmental egoism.' Now, with everyone working in one big office, he hopes the old power structure will disintegrate.

Oticon has also disposed of its desks. Now, every employee has a portable work station that he or she wheels to where they need to work that day. All the work stations are identical – a desk top, with no drawers and no personal effects, just the computer.

Staff have to be mobile, because their job roles are fluid, says Kolind. 'An engineer may be a superchip designer one day, but in another project, he'll do a market study or answer the phone.'

The fluid structure has made a big difference to individual

jobs. As one function manager says: 'I spend more time communicating with other employees, my job varies much more than previously and things are getting done much faster and smoother than before.'

The only compulsory task of the day is to read the company news and go through the mail, which has been opened in the early hours of the morning and scanned into the computer system. Material is computerized as part of Oticon's war on paper. 'We changed from pages of memos to talking to one another to get things done,' says Kolind. Important documents are now scanned into the computer and then shredded, along, of course, with all the unimportant ones. Now shredded memos and documents tumble symbolically through the company cafeteria.

As a result, says one secretary, 'the quality of my work has improved. I spend less time on trivial tasks like writing memos and photocopying – in short, less time on paperwork – and more time on improving my skills and using them on more qualified tasks.'

With details of every project and all financial data on the computer, any employee can learn the status of any current project within minutes, and get a complete picture of how the company is doing by spending half an hour at the screen.

Project leader Steen Davidson says this completely open information strategy makes possible whole new ways of organizing work. Projects themselves are no longer run across several departments. Instead each project remains a single entity with different specialists within it. Ever-changing project teams choose which jobs to handle and assign themselves tasks that interest them, and individual employees choose which projects they want to work on and can apply to work on any task where they think they can contribute usefully.

The system is not, however, as chaotic as it might look. Project heads are responsible for seeing ventures through, and each project has measurable objectives which are reviewed monthly and given a critical success level: minimal, acceptable, or, as often happens, splendid. And, to ensure that the dull work also gets done, everybody, from secretaries to managers, is obliged to take part in the less popular tasks, such as the major mailing the company undertakes twice a year.

At first, says Davidson, employees were uncertain about the new strategy. And, adds Kolind, 'some managers couldn't accept the fact that they were being monitored all the time by their staff.' Most however, have come round. 'Recently one secretary commented that it was much more interesting to work in this way and she preferred the set up to her former job,' says Davidson. This acceptance, however, was not easily won. The company spent six months demystifying the new strategy for employees, using group discussions and bringing in consultants to criticize the system and stimulate further discussion.

It's still not Utopia of course, but the problems are outweighed by the tangible gains of the new structure. Speed and creativity are the most immediately apparent – and badly needed. As a small company facing growing competition from multinational manufacturers, Oticon couldn't hope to gain a cost advantage. Kolind opted instead for a productivity advantage. 'The target of organizing Oticon in this manner was to improve productivity by 30 per cent within three years,' says Kolind. 'This target has now been reached and the time to market of our products has decreased by 50 per cent.'

Davidson says that they are giving the experiment 'from here to eternity' to succeed. Kolind, however, admits that it is just an experiment. If it does not work, they will return to the old system. This doesn't seem likely to happen soon, however: 'Our system may look to an outsider like a form of organized chaos,' says Kolind. 'But it's an organized chaos that works.'

NISSAN MOTOR GB LTD

In 1990, the Nissan Motor Company took the decision to set up a fully-owned company, Nissan Motor (GB) Limited (NMGB), to distribute cars and commercial vehicles in the UK. The new company had the ambitious aim of achieving 10 per cent of the UK market, and being recognized as the best vehicle distributor for customer care by the year 2000.

But NMGB not only had to become a company capable of achieving these things – it had to become operational in less than a year. A whole company and a whole dealer network had to be put in place between April and December 1991.

Says Anthony Eastwood, NMGB's personnel and general affairs manager:

> We knew that to set up the company and achieve the goals we'd set ourselves could only be done through people. We're a service company – we don't make anything – so while processes can be made more efficient, it's the people that are going to achieve things for you. The only way to succeed, then, was to set up a company in which employees had the latitude and ability to achieve our far-reaching objectives.

Eastwood and his colleagues proposed to set up, on NMGB's greenfield site, an empowered organization. Nissan's version of empowerment comprises four critical factors:

❑   an empowered culture

❑   a structure to support it

❑   the right people

❑   a system to maintain it.

'All four are needed to succeed and gain the benefits of an empowered workforce,' says Eastwood.

An empowered culture

'We wanted an organization where people could be trusted to make decisions, often with fairly sketchy background information, and make them correctly,' he says.

We looked to achieve a culture where the Japanese principle of Kaizen – continuous improvement – could be put into practice; where individuals are encouraged to continually evaluate the jobs they are doing and ask themselves whether the job could be done any better.

To do this, we needed both highly capable individuals and people who could work as part of a team, which are not always mutually compatible qualities. Above all, we needed flexibility from all our staff. People had to be prepared to do whatever was necessary to get the job done, but also recognize that demand on an individual role would change over time.

The teamworking culture is sometimes difficult for managers and supervisors, especially when there is a tight deadline to meet. He adds: 'Sometimes they have to bite their lips and achieve things through their teams, rather than taking the authority back and doing it themselves.'

NMGB does not run specific training courses on empowerment. 'We see empowerment as a gradual process and not something that can be covered in a training course. However, training in general is an important part of developing an empowered culture, and we take our empowerment drive into account when setting up courses,' says Eastwood.

Structure

The structure put into place to engender this culture involves many of the elements common to most empowered companies.

First, there are no job descriptions. 'That doesn't mean that employees don't know what they have to do,' says Eastwood.

We have a comprehensive performance management system which enables employees and their managers to agree exactly what's required. However, we felt that giving everyone a formal job description would inhibit the flexibility we were trying to engender. By saying to someone: 'You will do A, B and C', the inference is 'you won't do E, F and G'. Everyone has to be prepared to do whatever is necessary to meet the company requirements. We haven't got time for demarcation disputes.

NMGB's structure is also very flat. Everyone has one of five job titles and even those are not hard and fast – there is some overlap between the grades. 'A lot of companies in this country are currently de-layering, trying to move towards a less hierarchical structure. We had the advantage, starting from scratch, that we were able to design a flat organization rather than having to go through the sometimes painful process of removing layers of management,' says Eastwood.

'As you might expect with a small number of grades, each one covers a wide range of responsibilities,' he adds.

> We have administrators who are responsible for managing contracts worth hundreds of thousand of pounds with external agencies. Similarly, if the manager is the best placed person to run off 200 photocopies, then the manager is the person who does it. Each employee has the scope to expand his or her responsibilities and to develop their role in the best way they see fit to achieve their objectives.

NMGB also wanted to ensure that flexibility was not inhibited by cumbersome rules and procedures, so it has tried to keep the amount of bureaucracy to an absolute minimum.

> Obviously it's unavoidable in some areas, but, in the same way we don't give individuals job descriptions, we also try to avoid producing detailed documents on how they should do their jobs. We think our employees are sufficiently bright that they can work out the best ways for themselves. After all, they know the job better than anyone else. Similarly we try to keep our internal communications as informal as possible. If someone's got something to say to a colleague, they're encouraged to say it, not send out a snotty memo copied to all and sundry.

The physical work environment, in open plan offices, is also designed to promote flexibility. Says Eastwood: 'Again we had the advantage of new premises specifically built for this purpose. But while you need open plan offices to develop the sort of atmosphere that we are attempting to achieve, they're not enough in themselves. It's open plan minds you need more than anything else.'

People

NMGB managers make a point of recruiting such open plan minds. 'The structure and the people have to fit each other, so it was important that we recruited people we felt could fit with our empowered culture and structure,' says Eastwood.

At NMGB, this means, among other things, people who are well qualified. Over a third of employees are academically or professionally qualified to graduate level or equivalent. 'We very rarely take someone on just to do a specific job – we're looking for someone who has the ability to carve out a long term career for themselves at Nissan,' he says.

> We also look for people who are capable of thinking outside of any traditional approach to a job, who are open minded and ready to take on a challenge. This is absolutely essential if you are to have an empowered organization. Some people are not really interested in taking on more responsibility, or in coming up with new ideas. They want to come to work, do a day's work, and go home again. There's nothing wrong with that in itself and some organizations rely on people like that. But in an organization such an NMGB, we need people who are willing and able to think for themselves.
>
> It may seem slightly surprising, but we also look for people with motor industry experience. In an ideal world, it would have been nice to be able to take on lots of people from outside the industry who were untainted by the dyed-in-the-wool traditions that can characterize this sector. However, as we had only about nine months to set up a fully functioning company we needed people who knew the industry, especially in the more senior positions.

NMGB recruiters also like to let potential employees know what they are getting themselves into: 'We make it quite clear what our culture is and that a flat structure inevitably means that you won't get a promotion every year. We may lose a few good candidates as a result, but it does mean that we get people who are comfortable with the Nissan way of operating,' says Eastwood.

A system to maintain it

What binds NMGB's structure together is its Performance Management System (PMS). This links individual activities to the objectives of the business; it also helps make the difference between a team of empowered people pulling together to meet business objectives, and a group of employees freed to please themselves.

PMS, simply put, links individual objectives to company objectives. 'Employees need to be aware of what the company is trying to achieve, and what role each department has to play in that, so that everyone is able to take decisions in the best interests of the company,' explains Eastwood.

The performance management system ensures there are clearly defined targets and objectives at both organizational and individual level, and a system to check whether, and how well, they have been achieved.

First, top management sets organizational level targets and objectives. These are then communicated to all employees, not just the senior managers. 'This level of communication is essential in an empowered company. Employees must know where the goal posts are, what the organization is striving to achieve, and through this develop an understanding of the contribution they need to make,' says Eastwood.

There continues a cascade of objectives, with each employee agreeing what their part in fulfilling the objectives will be: Directors agree the part their function will play in achieving corporate objectives; managers agree with their directors how their department will help achieve functional objectives; and individual employees agree with their managers the part they will play in achieving departmental objectives. This, says Eastwood, is not an especially new or radical approach, but it has been successful, for three reasons:

❑ PMS emphasizes agreed objectives: individual, departmental, functional and corporate objectives are not assigned from on high. Rather, they are all agreed by the people responsible for meeting them.

❑ PMS involves self-appraisals: individuals assess how well they have met their objectives, as well as being appraised by their managers.

❑ The company's directors and managers have bought into the system. 'The management team were an integral part of the consultation process on the new scheme,' says

Eastwood. 'Directors and managers attended a one day training programme to ensure a consistent way of carrying out the appraisals. This may not seem such a big feat, but we all know how hard it is to get senior managers on training courses.'

NMGB is already profiting from empowerment, says Eastwood:

The main benefit has been achieving our sales objectives. We are, after all, in the business of selling cars. The other major advantage has been the creation of a dynamic and stimulating business environment with most employees motivated by the fact that the achievement of their individual objectives, through teamwork and flexibility, has contributed to the overall organization's achievements. Within this environment, we can tackle our goals over the coming years with a great degree of confidence.

Besides, if we hadn't done it the empowered way, we probably couldn't have done it at all. We certainly wouldn't have attracted the high calibre of employees we now have to be able to effectively promote the ethos of continuous improvement.

BRITISH MARITIME TECHNOLOGY

In 1992, Andrew Tyler, a 24-year-old marine scientist at British Maritime Technology (BMT), developed a new oilspill information system. Product development wasn't in his job description, neither was marketing or promotion; but he's now in charge of all aspects of marketing and developing the new system. He is, in BMT's language, championing it.

'I don't think I would have been given this much freedom and responsibility anywhere else,' says Tyler, now 26 and head of technology and business development in BMT's Marine Information Systems Group. 'BMT is a company that gives one an extremely long leash, and they judge on results, not job title or age.'

But as little as five years previously, championing a new idea at that level in BMT would have been 'totally impossible,' says Andrew Docherty, BMT's director of corporate services. 'There would have been far too many layers of bureaucracy to get through. The organization simply wasn't set up to allow someone to do that.'

BMT has seen some dramatic changes since it started to shed its bureaucratic shackles in 1985. That year, the National Maritime Institute (NMI), a government laboratory that had just been privatized, and the British Ship Research Association (BSRA) merged to form BMT, a private company set up to market commercial consultancy, contract research and software to maritime markets.

The new organization inherited considerable assets in terms of people, resources and advanced know-how, and was expected to stand on its own financial feet after a period of transitional, but rapidly reducing, government funding. However, little thought seemed to have been given to the fact that both organizations had previously been allocated work by their parent bodies, and had not yet had a chance to find other clients.

It was a difficult transition, says Tyler: 'It has taken a lot longer to move from a public to private company than anybody would have thought.'

By 1988 BMT was in a state of crisis. 'We came very close to going out of business. Our long-term future was very much in question; and the transitional funding provided by the government was coming to an end. The sky was going to fall in if we didn't do something,' says Docherty.

At the beginning of 1989 BMT was entirely restructured. A holding company, British Maritime Technology Group, was formed to manage the group's financial assets. The rest of the business was divided into six wholly-owned subsidiary companies, each with its own board and the freedom to determine and plan its own strategic future. The marketing, finance and personnel functions were also largely devolved to the subsidiaries. This left the BMT Group head office lean, with a role limited mainly to guidance and advice rather than control, and only about 20 of BMT's 450 staff.

The subsidiaries cut several layers out of their management structures too. Most of BMT's operating companies now have, besides their board, only one layer of management to whom all staff report. 'We also tried to relate individuals as closely as possible to the work they did and to their customers. For the first time, staff at each location, dependent on the performance of their own company, realized that their contribution was crucial to their own success and prosperity,' adds Docherty.

The majority of BMT's employees are technically qualified to at least graduate level, and they expect to be treated as capable of contributing to the success of the business – recognition that was largely denied them under the old command and control structure. Now, everyone at BMT is encouraged to take on new responsibility and to operate as mini business managers in charge of small projects or discrete elements of a larger project. The project structure of much of the work also gives people experience in working with staff of different disciplines, backgrounds and personalities.

There are opportunities to run much bigger businesses as well. The average company size of 20 to 100 employees is accepted as the maximum practical size by most BMT managing directors – anything larger begins to dilute the benefits. Managing directors whose companies achieve this size, or see a part of their business starting to grow out of proportion in a particular market, prefer to hive off the activity into a separate stand-alone business.

'The incentive this provides to staff is obvious,' says Docherty. 'They know that if their efforts are successful, they may be given the opportunity to run their own show.' New business opportunities are given to a 'champion' to develop them, with the prospect of managing the business if it proves successful. These start-up operations can call on the available resources of the BMT Group to help them, but they are free to choose the direction they wish to take.

BMT's empowered culture and flat structure also mean that staff can take on a lot of responsibility very early in their careers. 'We are not going to say "You're only 23. It's not possible." If someone has the ability, we let them have a go. Our experience has been that in these circumstances capable staff thrive and develop more quickly,' says Docherty.

This has certainly been the case for Andrew Tyler: 'I was given responsibility for whole projects lock, stock and barrel after only one year in the company,' he says.

> With the oil spill system I developed, the company underwrote the development costs, but left me alone to get on with it. If I feel I need, for marketing reasons, to make a trip to the Far East, I'll just go. I'll have to justify it in terms of new business at the end of the year, but I don't have to fill out forms in triplicate to arrange it ahead of time. Anywhere else, I would have to go through layers and layers of management to get things done.

All pay at BMT is performance-related. The overall performance of each company dictates how much money can be made available for pay increases and this is the only element, which is subject to approval by the group board. Profit sharing is part of a further drive to give all staff a real sense of participation in the business.

Performance-related pay has paid off, says Docherty:

> Staff who find their skills are inadequate in a particular area are quick to press for training to eliminate weaknesses or develop new skills. Where a company is performing badly, the staff are much more aware of the need to make improvements, as problems are seen as direct threats to their own prosperity. Change, therefore, becomes an issue that everyone is interested in achieving. And, if this demands that individuals take on new roles, they at least understand why it is necessary.

There was some resistance to increased participation, however, says Docherty:

> Like any change, it was unsettling, and it was especially difficult for some of the technical staff. They had been used to being somewhat removed from the customers, but now they had to take responsibility for customer service because the layers of management that used to shield them had disappeared. They could no longer say 'I just do the calculations, someone else can take care of the commercial aspects'. There are some people whose attitudes have not yet changed, but most have responded very well to the increased responsibility.

It's also been the case that different operating companies have changed at different paces:

> Those that have been financially successful since the reorganization have moved towards empowerment more quickly, because they have seen that it works; those that are still struggling, for example because they operate in a more depressed market, can see the benefits but haven't taken to empowerment as wholeheartedly.

Each operating company is also free to choose how empowered it wants to be. 'We don't impose a structure on our subsidiaries,' says Docherty. 'The basic elements, like the flat structure, the payment for performance and releasing the potential of staff exist throughout the group, but beyond that each operating company has a personality of its own. They operate in different markets, and have different needs.' BMT Group policy is to be flexible and allow each operating companies to develop the structure and systems that works best for it.

A critical lesson that BMT and the people within it have learned since the restructuring is that participation and involvement cannot be commanded.

Another is that change has to come from the top: 'You need a CEO who basically trusts people, who believes that people should be given opportunities and is prepared to let a few things go wrong,' says Docherty.

But no one at BMT set out with these ideas in mind, he adds:

We don't have a philosophy of empowerment. We just do it. We arrived at the way we operate because of the beliefs of a few individual managers, by trial and error, by pure chance and, to some extent, through desperation.

In 1989, we thought that if anything could work this would be it, and we were prepared to experiment, because things could hardly have got worse. Perhaps our biggest incentive was a fight for survival.

COLGATE

In 1990, the management team at Colgate UK, a subsidiary of the toiletries multinational Colgate Palmolive, set itself a challenge – to create a team-based organization at the company's Salford site as rapidly as possible.

The first task was to provide staff with the techniques they needed to problem-solve in multiskilled teams. A one week training course, run by the Coverdale Organization, a consultancy specializing in teamworking skills, gave 100 staff from various functions sufficient problem-solving skills to start up a number of ad hoc teams.

The first group – a mixed team of accounts and operations staff – set up a project team to tackle the factory's inefficient manual purchase order system. The team's job was to iron out problems in preparation for transfer to an on-line computer system. 'Using the skills they'd learned on the course, the accounts and operations people worked successfully together,' says John Nicholls, Colgate's Continuous Improvement Manager.

Throughout 1991 and into 1992, people in all parts of the factory learned, and used, the new problem solving and teamworking techniques. Ad hoc cross-functional teams sprung up, to tackle, among other things, new product launches.

The teamwork approach worked – so well, in fact, that Colgate management opted to run its new greenfield manufacturing site entirely on a teamwork basis.

In 1992, the company launched a project to start up a new manufacturing plant at its Mouthrinse Focus Factory. 'Mouthrinse is one of our newest product developments,' says Nicholls. 'We decided to start the new manufacturing plant from scratch with empowered cross-functional teams and, for the first time, we extended the teamwork approach to the shopfloor level.'

Thirty technicians, from both the existing plant and from outside the company, were recruited for the new site. 'At one time we would have called these people line operators,' says Nicholls.

They would have had limited responsibility, with foremen and supervisors as their superiors. But we changed their title to technician because we wanted to develop the idea that the technician is ultimately responsible for the whole job. We also wanted to help them develop the skills they needed to do that.

Now, the technicians are expected, and are being trained, to work as both line operators and mechanics – jobs which previously had been separate – and team members decide who does which job.

Working in teams, the technicians tackled a number of projects and tasks that had to be completed before the plant could open. With the help of some specialist support staff, such as engineers, the teams divided the tasks among themselves so that the site could start operation within a tight, five month deadline. Now, says Nicholls,

the plant has been operating for a year and we have started a second production line. The new mouthrinse line has been a success in terms of quality and flexibility. Though, like any line that has just begun operation, it has not reached its performance potential yet. In most start up operations there is a high risk of major safety problems too, but significantly this line had an extremely good safety record.'

It has an excellent staff retention record as well: of the 30 recruits, 28 are still with the company, and absenteeism runs at 4 per cent – half the company average.

Staff had mixed reactions to the empowerment idea, however, says Nicholls.

Some technicians prefer the new system and adapted quickly to becoming both a line operator and a mechanic; others preferred to remain specialist. There will always be people who will find teamworking and multiskilling difficult to adapt to. Usually it is the line operators with a lower level of basic skills, who see more benefits from the new working regime, while some mechanics are unhappy about a perceived loss of status.

Eventually, Colgate aims to have the technicians handle procurement and production schedules, and spend only 60 per cent of their time on the line. They will also be responsible for project work, training, and assessing and commissioning new equipment.

Colgate also experimented with the idea of a single pay system, to encourage the concept of a single status team. 'But we found it was important to recognize the skills of the electricians and mechanics who provide a major contribution, so we are redesigning the pay system to account for that,' says Nicholls.

The teamworking concept is not an experiment, however. The company plans to extend it to most areas of the original Salford site, starting with the dental cream filling and packing lines, which will adopt technician team-based working.

One of the biggest advantages of the new approach is the way teams can sort out problems among themselves, says Nicholls. One telling example occurred in 1992, when Nicholls wanted ten technicians to go to Germany on a fact-finding mission. 'It meant a week off site and everybody thought they had a reason to go,' he says. 'So we gave them a choice: either they chose ten candidates from among themselves, or the managers would decide instead. In the end, the team selected ten technicians to make the trip and this group brought back some very useful information.' The act of selecting the team was useful in itself, he adds:

> By working it through, the technicians learnt a lot about interpersonal skills. They looked at why people were going, who were the best people to go, and who had the best understanding of the issues involved. The argument went on for several hours, but it introduced them to consensus decision-making and the concept of buying into the final result.

Another advantage of the new system is that people at Colgate can now pull together teams at much shorter notice than ever before. 'If, for example, we have some new business and a tight schedule in which to work, we know we can call people together from across the site and work through the problem with the common language we've learned,' says Nicholls. 'Now, we can set out a task, define its purpose and use a systematic approach to tackle the problem.'

HARVESTER

Harvester, a 78-strong chain of branded restaurants, removed hierarchy in the space of a year within the framework of a highly structured system implemented from its headquarters. Harvester staff are now empowered, within a tight framework, challenging targets, and clear accountabilities, to handle a much wider range of responsibilities.

The change began in November 1990, when the chain restructured into a flat non-hierarchical organization. There are now two layers between the managing director and the frontline personnel who look after the guest.

Stephen Evans, managing director, explains,

> Its not enough to empower only the managers, you have to empower everybody at the same time. To turn an organization into an empowered one you have to make clear that this change is going to happen and then do it all at once. You have to go for it and really trust people.

In order to restructure effectively Harvester had to:

❑ de-layer to the minimum amount of layers that can be made individually and clearly accountable

❑ restructure the remaining layers into multi-functional self-managing teams

❑ create a value-driven organization that achieves its purpose

❑ set up effective systems that support the organization's structure and values.

The key systems are:

1. Communication.

2. Appraisal.

3. Reward.

4. Recognition.

5. Promotion – one of the biggest problems with the flat structure is promotion, as it is perceived that opportunities are taken away. Harvester have set up a horizontal

promotion programme, which ensures that at any point anyone can be promoted on merit and not have to wait for someone to move on.

6. Measurement of sales and profit output.

7. Measurement of quality.

To de-layer, it was vital to identify the critical job roles. The exercise was carried out starting with those interfacing with the customer (Harvester calls them guests). This identified the tasks necessary in the organization to get the job done. It was imperative that no accountabilities were shared, although everyone is responsible to a greater or lesser extent. 'Accountabilities are what the individual must do or make happen and what the job holder is judged by in output terms. Everyone has one or more accountabilities which can include recruitment, drawing up rotas and keeping track of the sales targets in the restaurant (as opposed to the kitchen or the bar),' Diane Ashness, human resources director explains.

A typical example of this is that only one person, the brand manager, is accountable for the Harvester menus. He is empowered to change the menu, and no committee signs it off. This means one person has full responsibility for making the menus work not just for the guest but also through suppliers. When Harvester was looking for a new supplier for a particular brand of bread, it found a baker in the Midlands who could supply the exact requirement. Unfortunately, it was then found that this regional baker did not have a distribution system to enable it to deliver to all 78 Harvesters, and was therefore considering declining the business. At that point, Harvester's brand manager suggested that the baker might like to talk to the company which supplied fresh vegetables and which carried out daily deliveries around the country; as a result these two suppliers have worked out an arrangement whereby joint deliveries are now made.

There are now four layers: the front-line team members, the team manager, the regional manager and the executive director. Three of the four layers are based on self-managing teams. The only layer that is not is the team manager, who is a line report to the regional manager. Head office has support teams for personnel, training, business development, sales and commercial, and these have various accountabilities to deliver.

Starting with the people closest to the guest, there are teams in the restaurant, pub, kitchen and in some cases accommodation. These teams are joined together to make up a Harvester team.

Explains Bernard O'Neill, manager of the Globe Tavern in Dulwich:

> We don't have staff, we have team members. Each member has different responsibilities, so one of our waitresses, Vanessa, is team expert on children; another, Halinka, has a special responsibility for family days.

Each team on each shift has a coordinator. The coordinator makes the snap decisions which are necessary in the fast-moving atmosphere of a packed restaurant. Nobody is appointed to take this job permanently; instead, all team members at different times will fulfil this role. Whoever is accountable for the rotas in that team decides who is to be the coordinator on a particular shift.

The branch teams are responsible for recruitment and promotion. Each branch has a coach who handles all training and some other personnel issues. This leaves marketing and going out into the community to get business to the branch manager. The manager also acts as facilitator, encouraging people to believe they can organize themselves in this new way. Even the responsibility of opening up, traditionally a manager's job, is shared by appointed people.

The next team is at regional level and is made up of 25 Harvesters. This team is not so interdependent, but members nevertheless meet regularly to learn from one another. The aim is to recognize and celebrate success, as well as to encourage other team members, who are not contributing, to improve and achieve. A great deal of work is carried out instilling a sense of pride in each regional team in what it is contributing to the overall Harvester brand. Each regional team is supported by a mini head office with a team leader, a training manager, control manager and secretary. They have their own identity and office, and are accountable for delivering their part of the bargain to the Harvester.

Personnel turnover rose in the first six months after empowerment was brought in. The new regime was regarded as highly threatening by some of the existing Harvester people – not surprisingly, since many perceived they had lost status.

'Another element that contributed to the turnover was what we dubbed "The Pain Factor",' comments Andrew Jones, one of Harvester's regional team leaders. 'Although we can now all see the benefits, both personal and corporate, from our restructuring, it was not easy for some to make the transition from boss to leader, from being led to leading.' The attitude changes called for are illustrated by the following COPS planning model.

Harvester Restaurants COPs Planning Model

CULTURE

Theory X	Theory Y
Low quality concern	High quality concern
Closed and secretive	Open and trusting
Conservative and risk averse	Entrepreneurial
Low team spirit	High team spirit
Task orientation	Results orientation
Organizational focus	Guest focus
Status oriented	Meritocracy

ORGANIZATION

Top-down	Bottom-up
High role definition	Loose role definition
Static	Constantly changing
Serves employees	Serves guest
Line	Cluster
Formalized reporting procedures	Autonomous work groups
Competitive	Collaborative

PEOPLE

Unskilled	Skilled
Limited potential	Vast potential
Low commitment	High commitment
Reactive	Pro-active
Low organizational commitment	High organizational commitment
Antagonistic	Cooperative
Oppose change	Like change

SYSTEMS

Organization-led	Business-led
Rigid	Flexible
Inorganic	Organic
Hindrance	Supportive

For empowerment to be effective, Harvester's managing director Stephen Evans believes team members must use the restaurant chain's values to guide their actions. So everyone who joins the organization – whether head office personnel, unit managers, chefs or waitresses – is trained in the mission. Even the suppliers attend a one-day mission training session which examines the mission, values, commitments and benefits. At the mission training, Harvester uses videos which feature companies with a high level of commitment to customer services. These include Federal Express, Disney, United Airlines, Worthington Industries and McDonalds.

The attendees are then required to look at what the mission means to them. Waitresses and waiters look at the mission condensed into four key statements:

1. Our business is hospitality.

2. Our commitment is to help our people succeed.

3. We all ensure our guests enjoy their visits.

4. Their satisfaction guarantees growth.

They then decide how they will fulfil the declaration. Many decide to smile and make eye contact with every guest. Suppliers have suggested that they will arrange deliveries outside the critical 12 noon to 2pm lunchtime period. On visits to individual Harvesters, head office staff park in the parking spot furthest away from the restaurant's front door, so leaving the best places for the guests.

Harvester uses mystery guests to measure service quality; these are not outsiders, but team members from other Harvesters. 'There is an extra benefit from this,' explains Ashness, 'A member might return from a visit and say "I marked them down for that, but we're not so good at that either." Or they might pick up good ideas.'

The basis of Harvester's approach is that it trusts its people to move the business forward, and this seems to have paid off. People turnover has fallen 20 per cent since 1991/92. Recession might have influenced this figure, but Diane Ashness feels that taking out the assistant manager level and giving more responsibility to front-line people has helped.

She also believes that it is significant that the stability of core full-time people has increased. Sales have increased year on year since Harvester first went flat, despite the recession and more significantly, net operating profits have risen dramatically as a result of every team member being involved with what they have come to regard as their business.

Harvester recruits people who are sympathetic to its values. One of its core values is that the guest is the most important person within Harvester. Another core value is trust. Harvester trusts its people; when interviewing potential team members, the interviewer tries to find out if they buy into this value. If they come from an organization that starts from the assumption that everybody is stealing and then puts lots of rules in place to prevent this, the potential recruit may find it difficult to start trusting staff. The aim is to recruit people who can trust others and buy into all Harvester's values, then they will be able to operate in an empowered way within the organization.

It is not surprising that over and above the seven key systems, Harvester places the heaviest emphasis on the processes of selection, induction and training, both initial and ongoing. Given that applicants will be joining self-managing teams, it is seen as vital that members of that team are involved in the selection process – it is not a question of imposing a new team member on others but more a welcoming process if the person fits.

People wishing to join Harvester as potential team managers or coaches are invited to attend regular screening days, which include interviews with existing team managers. These are followed by attendance at a one-day assessment centre. Applicants who have not previously worked within the hospitality industry are also expected to complete a two-day on-the-job experience to help them understand the rigours of the industry before committing themselves to a career change.

The final stage is a partnership interview with the prospective line manager, guaranteeing commitment on both sides to an effective future working relationship.

This can all take two or three months, and may appear a long-winded way of appointing, but those offered a position are more likely to be the right choice and, more importantly, all team members are made to feel they own that choice.

Induction, depending on the position offered, can also be a lengthy process, particularly for team managers and coaches. Quite apart from them gaining the general and specific skills and knowledge of the restaurant business, they are thoroughly grounded in Harvester's mission and values – a process that continues to retirement. Harvester estimates that the initial cost of inducting a team manager averages £7,000 – so no wonder the selection process is so thorough. The chain see guest satisfaction as paramount and thus perceives combining job skills with personal commitment as a potent force for achieving this.

When Harvester were talking to consultants, the Tom Peters Group, about being a better service provider, they found they were better than they thought, and became an example for others to follow – in fact they were well on their way to a vision that there is 'a waiting list of quality people who want to join Harvester'.

NUCLEAR ELECTRIC

Nuclear Electric was forced into its change programme by the privatization of the electricity generating industry. The government planned to privatize Nuclear Electric alongside the other three companies, but in November 1989 the organization was withdrawn from the sale and asked to form a wholly government-owned company. It had been deemed that it was not economically viable to operate Nuclear Electric as a privately owned company.

In March 1990 Nuclear Electric became a plc without a much greater brief than to improve things. As Dr Clive Smitton, Change Programme Director, points out:

> It was a very unhappy situation. We had an able set of people who had previously been told they were the great hope for the future and produced the cheapest electricity. After Nuclear Electric had been withdrawn from the sale it was clear that it would be allowed to go to the wall if the company was not economic.

Privatization heralded a new age of intense competition in the electricity industry. Nuclear Electric was now competing directly with existing newly privatized non-nuclear generators, regional electricity companies moving into generation partnerships and new generators, especially those using low-cost gas fired plants.

Moreover, after Chernobyl, public opinion was very unfavourable to nuclear power. Nuclear Electric had to show the public that it understood their concerns about safety, and that its safety record was beyond reproach; and to demonstrate that nuclear power is cleaner than fossil fuels like coal and gas.

Adds Smitton,

> There was no doubt we had a crisis on our hands, but we had some very great assets, the greatest being our skills. We had the most skilled workforce in the UK and lots of enthusiasm to prove that Nuclear Electric could compete with fossil fuels.
>
> The first year was spent revising our strategy.

Nuclear Electric had inherited all of Britain's nuclear generating assets and 16 per cent of the electricity market plus a partly built power station at Sizewell B. Other planned stations were put on hold and there was to be no nuclear investment until 1994. By that date, nuclear power had to be shown to be safe and competitive. Until 1998, nuclear power was being subsidized by a levy of 10 per cent on fossil fuels electricity generation. In 1990, Nuclear Electric was producing electricity for 5p a unit while fossil produced it at 2p unit cost. The aim was to bring down the unit price and become a competitive supplier without the levy.

By 1993, the company had increased output by 50 per cent and improved production by 55 per cent, by March 1994 production had been improved by 90 per cent. Nuclear Electric had increased its share of the electricity market from 16 per cent to 22 per cent, and by 1995, it will be profitable without the levy. This radical turnaround was achieved by technical improvements to the plants and also through restructuring and empowering people.

Dr Smitton explains:

> We introduced profit centre working and reduced our staff from 14,500 to 9,500. We slimmed down to one headquarters and reduced our number of technology centres to one. We visited Nissan, Shell and BP, among others, to learn from them. We held workshops to diagnose in teams how to take the business forward. Station managers asked all their staff what to do. We decided that we wanted to push responsibility down to the lowest level, broaden the skill base and allow wider responsibility. We decided to try a few things out – not everything worked.
>
> We made it clear that every little detail did not have to be OK'd by station managers. So, for example, foremen could decide overtime, or people could send faxes without authorization. We also gave every manager a copy of *Zapp, the Lightening Power of Empowerment* by William Byham.

To drive through its programme, Nuclear Electric bought in management consultants Kinsley Lord in mid-1991. It focused its efforts on Wylfa on the Isle of Anglesey as a pilot for its eight older magnox reactors, and Hartlepool for the new generation of AGRs.

Tony Capp, manager at Hartlepool, informed his staff of the current situation by meeting small groups until the entire workforce was told. He then ensured they were regularly updated. Now TV monitors throughout the site broadcast a constant flow of information about the station's performance. Authority was pushed downwards and this was accompanied by a number of symbolic gestures. The blue overalls of the industrial staff and the white overalls of the engineers were replaced with a single colour. The partition separating the managers' dining room from the staff canteen was demolished and the parking spaces for senior management blow-torched out.

Setting clear and demanding targets for almost every task was one of the keys to the successful turnaround. As its Change Management Handbook, the document that details the way the company turned itself around, states,

> When we set challenging targets for outages, the statutory period when the turbine generators are shut down and maintained, and when those targets were met to the day, we realized the power of setting clear and ambitious targets. It was a common complaint that people were not delivering the performance needed of them. The simple fact is that no one had clearly explained what they wanted and why it was wanted. At every level of the organization with every sort of issue, the single most important success factor has been setting clear targets and seeking the involvement of staff.

At Hartlepool, a new way of participative working slowly emerged. Take, for example, the annual outage. Previously all preparation had been handled by the station manager together with the engineering staff, who, are, in effect the station's middle management. In 1992 an outage team was formed. This was cross-functional and had representatives from all levels, from mechanical fitters to senior engineers. The station manager only authorized spending and set completion targets. The newly formed team was sent to Sweden to watch how a similar shutdown was handled. They were then given the freedom to copy best practice. The results were impressive. The outage had previously taken 17 weeks. Now it only took 10. That seven weeks' additional generation bought in an extra £11.6 billion. The success of this initiative spurred on other projects.

A full-time team looked at procedures in all departments

and the potential gains of work restructuring. It focused on the fuel route – the path that fuel takes through the station from its first arrival to its eventual despatch for reprocessing. In its previous form, much of the process relied on the skills and services of staff from a range of different departments. Work often came to a halt for hours on end until someone from the relevant department was free to perform a 10 second task. After asking those involved and mapping out how the job actually got done, the project team brought together all the skills needed from the beginning of the process to the end. As a result an estimated 59,000 man hours a year were saved. Those on the team now claim a sense of ownership and boast of pre-empting the management.

The Handbook underlines this point:

> We found that if we truly empowered our teams – giving them targets, resources, information and responsibility – they could achieve significant results provided they are competent and well led. This was true of both project teams and permanent work teams who were prepared to put aside normal functional or hierarchical constraints to work on problems in a focused and committed way We found it was particularly important for teams to have responsibility for implementing their ideas, not just for recommending changes to management.

Many of those at the forefront of the programme admit to being sceptical at the start. It was only when they saw the 'wrong' sort of people getting involved, what one could describe as the 'management's yes men', that they realized they could lose out if they did not get involved themselves.

The broad theory of the redesign was that a large proportion of the work at any level could be done by the level immediately below it. Under the existing structure the industrial staff were prevented from doing this by demarcation between levels. As the skills of the industrial staff were broadened, they were then able to relieve the 180 engineers of distracting and repetitive work.

According to Nick Hasell, writing in *Management Today* (July 1993), 'Not all staff have been convinced. There is a sizeable lobby of those who dispute that gains in performance are the direct result of the programme (rather than the gradual removal of design faults) and rue the shift in power away from engineers to those with broader management skills.'

But Ian Tomlin, change leader at Dungeness B has a different story:

> I used to be a section head responsible for training. I reported to the resources manager who was a member of the management team led by the station manager. Pre-empowerment I couldn't authorize expenditure on my budget and had to get everything countersigned. Anything with the station's name on it had to be signed by the station manager. I lost a lot of time sending my staff to chase signatures. Post-empowerment I was allowed to sign for any expenditure and I handled a budget of a million pounds. This gave me tremendous job satisfaction. Before, I had felt demeaned by having to get all those countersignatures. The new regime also freed up managers who no longer had to sign piles of orders.

Lisa Jones, an off-site course administrator, has worked at Dungeness B for almost five years:

> When I'm bookng a course and accommodation, there are various booking forms that have to be filled in. Previously they had to be countersigned, but now I can sign them myself. This saves a lot of waiting around for people to sign. It also means that when travel agents or course administrators phone up they can speak to me and not my manager. The post is handed straight to me now. I feel much more in control and I enjoy having the responsibility.

MARRIOTT

During the late 1980s, a combination of increased competition in the global hotel market, an oversupply of hotel rooms in the US and tougher economic conditions led Marriott to look at how it could improve its market position.

The company recognized that success would not come from changing the product or offering cheaper prices, but from having better, more customer focused staff than its competitors. So, in 1987, Marriott began working on a total quality programme. The objective was to shift the company's existing customer service emphasis from a procedural to a 'whatever it takes' approach.

While Marriott knew what it wanted to achieve, and had started several initiatives, it did not have a road map on how to get there – so the company turned to its suppliers for advice.

During 1990, Marriott's most senior managers visited some of the company's suppliers, Milliken, AT&T, and Fed-Ex and looked at how their quality programmes worked. It was from these benchmarking studies and its existing experience that Marriott developed its own brand of TQM.

Marriott also looked carefully at factors which influenced customer perceptions of service in its hotels. One such factor is that guests primarily deal with doormen, housekeepers and waitresses, so the customer's view of the hotel and the company as a whole is generally formed by the behaviour of front-line staff.

It followed that service quality could be enhanced by giving greater responsibility to customer contact staff – so empowerment became one the key elements of Marriott's total quality programme. The formal process of change and training concentrated on three areas:

❑ creating enthusiasm among the staff to achieve clearly defined goals

❑ developing problem-solving skills

❑ developing company culture to accommodate continuous improvement rather than static performance targets.

The training was in three parts – TQM 1-3. TQM 1 was on ewpowerment. Selected staff attended off-site courses which comprised activities such as role play, workshops and discussions. Themes included psychology, motivation, coaching and correcting mistakes.

Staff in hotels were then trained by these trainers. Again, role play and exercises were the main approaches used. The purpose of empowerment was explained in terms of the guests, colleagues and Marriott as a whole.

Examples of TQM and empowerment in action are recorded and published in Share it, an in-house quality magazine. The publication details all significant achievements and helps to spread the word on TQM throughout Marriott. It also serves as an ideas exchange between hotels.

Empowerment gives all Marriott staff (associates) the responsibility to act for the benefit of the customer. It allows staff to take action to avert or solve problems, without having to gain approval from their manager or supervisor first. In this way most customer problems and complaints can be prevented, rather than put right once they occur. Where problems do arise, empowered staff can solve them without delay, and where appropriate make amends.

A situation which could cause a guest to leave with a bad impression of Marriott can be turned into a positive one, and enhance customer loyalty, if properly handled. It requires associates to understand the principles behind empowerment and to use judgement in deciding what action to take. New management procedures, staff training and a fundamental culture change were crucial, as was a sensitive approach to handling mistakes. Staff who misjudged situations, or who were over-zealous in making amends for minor problems had to be coached without discouraging them from taking the initiative again.

Empowerment requires trust and confidence – from managers and staff. The system assures associates that their ideas will be listened to, and that their actions will have the support of management.

Involving staff in the decision-making process enhances their self-worth within the organization, and can pay dividends in term of reduced costs and service improvements –

the staff who do the actual work often know better than their managers how procedures work 'on the ground', and can identify ways of streamlining them.

A recent example of this was at the London Marriott Hotel in Grosvenor Square: the problem involved the speedy removal of room service trays from bedroom corridors. Room service attendants were responsible for clearing trays, but it was difficult to keep the corridor clear at all times. A team of associates worked on the problem, researching the situation and developing solutions. The result was a change of responsibility so that all staff who see trays in the corridors remove them. To encourage staff to participate, each tray carries a sticker which is saved by the person retrieving the tray. These can be exchanged for a range of gifts, such as a bottle of wine, or dinner in the restaurant.

Not only did this speed up the removal of trays, it also reduced the time room attendants spent looking for trays, freeing them for other tasks. One associate summed it up: 'If you think your job isn't important, you're wrong. It's not the job which makes you important, it is the way you do it.'

Another element of the TQM was cross-training of associates. By training staff to perform several job functions within the hotel, Marriott found that staff are more motivated – by a greater variety, and in some cases more responsibility in their jobs. The hotel benefits from having a more flexible, better trained workforce.

Examples of empowerment in action are many and varied, and Marriott has used some examples in its advertising in the past year.

❏ A guest at a Washington DC area Marriott Hotel had been invited to join President Clinton on his morning jog. The guest had not anticipated this and did not have a track-suit or suitable footwear. It was late in the evening and the shops were closed, so a member of staff lent the guest his tracksuit and brand new running shoes. Suitably attired the guest joined the President early the following morning.

❑ Another guest at the Romulus Marriott in Michigan left a bag on the airport shuttle. He realized his loss on arrival in Miami, where he was due to join a cruise ship. He contacted an associate at the Miami Airport Marriott, who contacted her counterpart in Romulus. He in turn arranged for the bag to be flown on the next available flight, sent it to the airport and faxed the baggage claim to the Miami hotel. They collected the bag and forwarded it to the cruise ship in time for the guest's departure.

❑ A cleaner at the San Francisco Marriott Hotel overheard a guest complaining that he had lost 50 cents in a drinks vending machine. Without hesitation he gave the guest 50 cents from his own pocket, much to the surprise and satisfaction of the guest.

It was not really a case of relaxing the rules, more of a gradual change in culture. There are still guidelines on empowerment and quality. Welcoming suggestions was an important way of encouraging staff to think about their jobs and the effect they have on guests and their colleagues. Once staff began to think in a different way, it became easier for staff to understand empowerment and how they can improve a guest's service experience. Says one associate, 'I feel more like part of a team – I can make decisions and suggestions and I have the respect of my supervisor.'

As it became clear that managers and supervisors were working in new ways, this gradually helped change the behaviour and approach of individuals. An event in September 1992 added another dimension to the Marriott quality programme. At that time the company concluded a master franchise agreement in the UK with Scott's Hotels Ltd, and overnight 13 hotels changed their name from Holiday Inn to Marriott.

During the months leading up to and following the change, Scott's undertook extensive staff training and development, and adopted Marriott's 'whatever it takes' principles. A training programme concentrating on service to internal customers was developed, and a series of quality circles made up of individuals from all areas of the company were trained to train their colleagues on the quality process. Marriott's own trainers and staff were involved in training in the UK, and key Scott's staff spent time in the US, ensuring a seamless transition.

An undertaking as large and diverse as Marriott's quality initiative – their hotel portfolio alone comprises over 750 hotels in 22 countries – inevitably had to overcome a number of obstacles, such as initial resistance to change. Marriott first approached the problem from the bottom up – believing that if the most junior staff were able to work in a different way, this would give senior staff more confidence in the programme.

It became clear that a 'trickle down' from senior management was also required because staff had to see and believe that senior management were totally committed.

There was also some initial resentment of the time required in implementing the new initiative. Some staff saw time spent in problem-solving, meetings and training as in conflict with their existing work. This largely disappeared as the process progressed.

Though these were anticipated, there were pitfalls which had not been planned for – it was necessary to convince staff that it was not just the 'year's staff motivation programme', but an ongoing process of change.

Marriott's empowerment process has resulted in a more energized, creative, and forthcoming workforce. Ideas are flowing from staff in all the functions and at all levels. It has also had an effect on managers' roles, making them more people-oriented – empowerment does not fit with a dictatorial management style.

There is more work to be done in some areas – for instance, in maintaining consistency across all Marriott hotels. This is central to the Marriott brand – the same in-room amenities are available in San Francisco, Warsaw and Hong Kong, and this is important to business travellers.

Some hotels have introduced more service enhancements than others, so the challenge is to control initiatives at the most active hotels without dampening enthusiasm, and to help people at other places which are further behind catch up.

Quality is an ongoing process at Marriott with continuous staff training and development all around the world. The company is pursuing an aggressive international development programme – aimed at developing a presence in all of the world's major capitals. Quality is central to development decisions, whether new properties are to be managed by Marriott or franchise partners.

KIMBERLY CLARK — RELEASING PEOPLE POWER

Kimberly Clark's Service and Industrial Sector was formed after the corporation reorganized into business sectors which operated across Europe. After delving into current management theories, the Service and Industrial Sector's senior management decided on a new set of managing principles and then started to reorganize in line with their decision guidelines. In so doing, the sector moved towards an empowered organization almost overnight.

Kimberly Clark is a £7 billion worldwide corporation principally engaged in the manufacturing and marketing of a wide range of products for personal, business and industrial users. Its products include tissues; infant, child, feminine and incontinence products; industrial wipers; healthcare products; newsprint; printing papers; technical papers and even aircraft services and commercial air transportation.

The Service and Industrial business was one of four European market sectors formed in 1988. Previously, the corporation had run its business autonomously country by country. Brian Howes, President of the Service and Industrial Sector, now had to develop the business as a customer-based organization with fully integrated sales, marketing, distribution, manufacturing and development functions.

The new organization adopted a new framework. Three groups of teams were formed with three different foci: Firstly, a local focus with the sales and marketing group of teams; secondly, a group which concentrated on a pan-European view of manufacturing; and thirdly a group which took a global view of technology exploitation.

'We inherited more positives than negatives from the old organizational set up,' says Howes. 'Twenty five to thirty years operating in various markets meant that we had a bank of good people, some good market franchises and many shared values, including well instilled Quality Management Principles and an emerging consciousness of the importance of what had become known as World Class Manufacturing.

'We were also becoming aware that there were rapid changes occurring in the basis of competition. In the "World Class World" flexibility of the organization and more particularly of its people was seen to be fundamental to survival.

'I realized that staffing the organization was simple. Our great managing task was to undertake a cultural revolution, in which the power of our people became paramount. As I faced the opportunity, I realized that all the knowledge and experience about our customers, our manufacturing, our distribution, our systems, in fact about nearly everything that would make the business a success lay in the people, the employees. We set out to release this power.'

The management team and Brian Howes spent several days locked together to gather their thoughts. From that meeting they distilled the decision guidelines which were to form the cornerstones of everything that followed. Explains Howes, 'These principles are not unique, but they were chosen by us and they have bound us together in a common purpose until today.'

The decision guidelines are:

❑   meet and know your customers;

❑   continually add value to everything you do;

❑   innovate fast;

❑   delegate and involve people; really let go.

The management team removed the old hierarchy and replaced it with networks. Key action teams were formed in production, development, sales and marketing, support and logistics. The European organization of 1000 people was grouped into 100 teams. Team members formed their own networks and did not rely on these being proscribed by senior management. 'We likened an empowered team to an orchestra in which management provided the music, the team leader acted as conductor and the team members as the highly skilled instrumentalists.'

The theories were tested out at a new factory at Coleshill in North Wales. The principles even extended to the design and construction of the mill. It was designed to give teams a pride in their company and their workplace. Internally the building has been designed to promote teamwork — there are no walls between operating areas, offices are integrated into the workplace and not a separate building.

Within the mill, the process has been designed so that complexity is reduced and self managing teams can take full charge without unnecessary overhead. Spaces were marked out on the floor to show where the product had to go at different stages of the manufacturing process. The teams knew they had made enough when stock storage areas, known as Kan Bans, were full. When they were empty the team knew they had to carry on producing. (Kan Ban is a just-in-time (JIT) term, and in fact the whole mill was running on a JIT system. The teams were also operating a preventative maintenance system.)

Training was particularly important for a group destined to run a £30 million plant. The teams started training six months before start up. Their training included quality management courses and outdoor activities to help team members realize their roles in the team. Employees are known as manufacturing team members and work on a shift system. They do not do paid overtime and are paid an annual salary. The aim is to remove the differentiation between hourly paid workers and staff. There are 20 support staff for 100 manufacturing team members.

At its new Business and Technology Centre in Northop, North Wales, the company has also striven to create an empowering environment. Again, there are no closed offices, open planned areas create an interactive environment and there are plenty of meeting rooms for networking and team sessions. Four people provide secretarial support to forty. Says Howes, 'They are considered equal members of the team. They are not subordinate. Their job is office management and purchasing as well as producing letters and visuals. For empowerment to work you can't load people down with a lot of bureaucracy so we use electronic mail a lot to eliminate excess paperwork.'

As the new processes have proved effective in the greenfield sites, the other factories have adopted many of the work practices.

Howes freely admits that Kimberly Clark is still developing its ideas. He explains 'We started with:

❑   Set high standards and help people achieve them.

246 THE POWER OF EMPOWERMENT

Then we moved on through the ideas of:

❑ employee involvement;

❑ using trained flexible people as the principal means of adding value;

❑ empowerment.

Today we talk about:

❑ Releasing self motivation by involvement, liberating energy and rewarding initiative.'

To reinforce empowerment, Kimberly Clark's Service and Industrial Sector removed the trappings of power, which management believed were intimidating and demeaning to the extent that they have no place in a teamworking environment. Out went titles, privileged parking, imposing offices, directors' dining rooms, overbearing behaviour and other status indicators. Instead, the management concentrated on eliminating bureaucracy. Everybody was encouraged to decide whether a meeting was important or not and if they decided it was not, they could then decide not to attend.

Reports were carefully scrutinized to see if they were really necessary. Sometimes reports had been compiled and written, yet had been used by nobody. This wasteful practice has largely stopped. People were asked to consider whether every bit of paper that landed on their desk was useful to them. If they decided that a particular document was no longer of any relevance to them, they were encouraged to make sure that they no longer received it.

Levels of management were eliminated, levels of training were increased and the company provided some guarantee of employment for contributors. At the same time, people were encouraged to concentrate on the customer as a source of strength rather than focusing inward towards the organization.

Since the changes, according to Howes, the Service and Industrial Sector has become a more productive, customer-oriented, flexible, enthusiastic organization, which has been a pleasure to lead.

Over the past five years several problems have raised their heads. For example, should team leaders be appointed or should leadership rotate according to the subject under discussion? Explains Howes, 'The answer may depend upon the stage of the team's development or the maturity of the team members. As we have moved towards self appraisal, we have recognized that some people continue to need more direction and coaching and I am now a supporter of the four stages of empowerment approach: From the team member being directed by his or her team leader, then coached, then supported and finally empowered.

'Full empowerment is achieved only when the team members are judged to be competent. This may sound obvious but it does not always happen in practice.'

After five years, Kimberly Clark conducted a survey of team members to see whether the programme was perceived as successful — 59 per cent now feel somewhat or strongly empowered. Strangely, the managers feel more empowered than their teams. Unlike in manufacturing and development areas where people tend to work closely in teams — in the field salesforce, which is often more individual and directive, the feeling of empowerment is not yet so well developed.

Verbatim comments from the team leader of the sales and marketing team in Germany give further insights on how to implement empowerment:

❑ The process needs a driver at the top for four or five years.

❑ Middle managers attempt to maintain power for a long time.

❑ Alternative means of career progression are needed.

❑ Status symbols do not die.

❑ Empowerment needs continual reinforcement and ongoing support.

❑ Teams must identify with the outcome of their activities and be incentivized accordingly.

Kimberly Clark managers also face the challenge of replacing hierarchy with an alternative form of career progression.

The company has established career development teams to provide a framework for personal career development. Individuals can progress up the ladder based on their skill and value to the organization.

One of the interesting difficulties faced was the unexpected problem of interfacing an empowered organization with a less advanced organization. Enthused, empowered team members with the light of conversion in their eyes constantly bounced off their less enlightened colleagues and encountered:

❑ mistrust;

❑ annoyance;

❑ impatience;

❑ resentment.

The other area where Kimberly Clark's Service and Industrial Sector is still struggling to find an answer is that of incentives. Currently the debate is one of balance — balance between profit sharing or payments made based on the success of the business or business unit, and incentives based on achievement of specific short-term objectives.

'In the early days, we believed that teams had to have common reward to work well together,' says Howes. 'Now, the teams are encouraged to evaluate themselves. They agree their own objectives, measure them, then report at the end of the year. The bonus is based on a percentage of salary.

'The problems arise when dozens of teams set themselves different objectives. This can cause dissension. Management has to oversee and judge the equity of objectives between different teams. In an attempt to solve the problem, we are now making objectives bigger rather than smaller teams. It is fairer if we organize incentives on a wider scale, with teams of forty rather than six. But we have to make sure that the individual still feels that he or she has an influence on the team.

'We are trying to create an environment where people take a much more active interest because they believe it will affect their own well being.'

One thing the managers at Kimberly Clark's Service and Industrial Sector are certain about is that incentives of some sort are essential to focus team effort. 'Individuals and teams must clearly identify with the end product — otherwise empowerment becomes increasingly hollow,' says Howes.

'For my own organization, I believe that the changes we have made are for the good. I would hate to be facing today's competitive market with a hierarchical, bureaucratic organization. I truly believe that empowerment has been the key to the success of the cultural revolution which we have been undertaking and will provide the flexibility to enable us to be more competitive in future.

'In my experience there are five cornerstones of empowerment, each of which is vital to successful implementation:

- An understanding of the business strategy;
- the establishment of clear guidelines;
- the availability of information;
- individual skill;
- reward focused on team results.

CHIAT/DAY

If an advertising agency is the place to find creative solutions, a Californian ad agency can be counted on for something completely off the wall.

That's what is happening at Chiat/Day, a Los Angeles-based agency that has turned its organizational structure literally inside out.

In 1976 Chiat's chairman Jay Chiat abolished formal offices and introduced open plan cubicles, even for top management. Now he has disposed of the cubicles — as well as the desks, phones, terminals and the filing cabinets.

Staff now spend their time working where they need to. That could be with a client in one of Chiat's project/meeting rooms, each is dedicated to a particular client; at one of the ad hoc shared work stations; at home; or even in their car. Increasingly, however, staff are encouraged to spend time at client's offices. 'We want them focused on the client's business, not internal issues of who has the better office,' Chiat told the *Financial Times*.[1]

This mobility is made possible largely by Chiat/Day's creative use of technology. Instead of fixed phones, each staff member has a mobile phone, each with its own number, and a notebook computer instead of a fixed terminal. Project file and company information is all scanned into the computer and accessed at a central library,

Chiat calls the new structure 'team architecture,' and hopes it will encourage more interactions between staff members, leading to better teamwork and creativity. He also expects it to have a financial payoff, because the agency needs less office space to accommodate its staff.

Team architecture and the work style that supports it is, he says, to a traditional office environment what a college is to a school. Instead of sitting at their desks all day, subject to close supervision, staff are free to go away and complete tasks as they see fit.

Chiat acknowledges, however, that such a radical change can be risky: 'The change is monumental. I don't think any of the people implementing it have any sense of how much trauma there's going to be and the period of time it is going to take for people to feel comfortable with this concept.'

He does, however, expect they will come to accept it.

References

1. Dickson, M., 'Dismantling the office,' *Financial Times*, 28 January 1994.

Index